W9-BDL-164

Budget Cooking ❖ *Elegant Dining*
The Kosher Experience

by Sue Epstein

PITSPOPANY PRESS

NEW YORK ❖ JERUSALEM

Text Copyright © 1996 Sue Epstein
Published by PITSPOPANY PRESS
Design: Laser Pages Publishing Ltd.
Cover Photo: Max Richardson
Illustration: Betty Maoz

All Rights Reserved.

ISBN: 0–943706–62–9
Printed in Hungary

For my grandchildren:

Sara, Binyamin, Moshe, Rina, Batsheva, Srulie, Eli, Avrum…
and all the ones to come.

You're what it's all about.

Budget Cooking ❖ Elegant Dining

The Kosher Experience

Table of Contents

INTRODUCTION

Almost all of us look for ways to economize on our food budget at one time or another, hopefully without compromising taste or quality. Whether you're on your own for the first time, retired, newlywed, or have a large family to cook for; whether you're naturally budget-conscious, or simply have too much month left at the end of your money — this cookbook is for you!

Budgeting is not a talent you're born with — it is something learned. Anyone can master the art of creative budgeting. When you use the recipes in this book, your friends and family won't even realize you're budgeting. Even with today's prices, you can eat-well-for-less with just a little bit of planning and creativity. Remember, inexpensive does not have to mean inferior.

Over many years of extensive and successful entertaining, I have learned that the atmosphere you create is as important as the foods you serve. While I've hosted many happy occasions where the menu consisted of whole poached salmon and other expensive ingredients, I've made equally enjoyable dinners where the menu was a simple spaghetti and garlic bread.

Friends invited to your home look forward to being with you. Yes, they also look forward to having a good meal, but it's not how expensive a cut of meat you serve, it's the memory of the atmosphere and company you create that remains with them long after the party is over.

Budgeting also doesn't mean that you'll never eat a sizzling steak or a succulent roast again. There will be times when you'll find steak on sale for the same price you usually pay for ground beef, or decide that the occasion warrants pulling out all the stops, regardless of the budget. And there will also be times when you'll want to try a certain dessert that may call for expensive ingredients.

Moderation is the key. If you're going to splurge on an expensive roast for a special occasion, watch your budget more carefully the rest of the week or month. If you want to try the expensive dessert, by all means go for it! But try to compensate by serving a more moderately priced appetizer and main course.

Remember too, that a recipe is just a guideline. When you make a recipe for the first time, try to follow directions as closely as possible. If you don't follow the recipe, and you aren't happy with the results, you won't know if it's that particular recipe or the changes you made to it that you didn't like. After you've tried the recipe, feel free to experiment and change it to suit your taste.

Be creative! Anyone with the ability to read and follow a recipe can become a fairly competent cook. Add some experience and creativity to that and you have the makings of a great cook. Good cooking also doesn't necessarily mean new and costly ingredients. Think about what you can put together with the bits of cheese saved in the freezer, or the gravy and meat scraps leftover from the roast you cooked, and the broken or stale pieces of cake that nobody ate.

I hope by the time you finish reading this book you will have gained some new ideas. Don't be afraid of a few failures. If your first effort at something is a disaster, try to figure out what happened and get right back in the kitchen and keep cooking.

Don't be afraid to write in your cookbook. Space has been provided for you to make notes about any changes or comments you may have. Nothing is worse than creating a delicious dish and then finding you can't repeat your triumph because you can't remember exactly what you did to the recipe. My own cookbooks are filled with comments about changes, substitutions I made, who I served and how they liked it.

Whether you cook because you enjoy it or because it's something that you can't get out of, you want to feel that the time you've spent in the kitchen has been worth the effort.

Your attitude about cooking is equally as important as the recipe. Very few of us want to spend endless hours in the kitchen. People today want to spend their time studying, playing tennis or a dozen other things, yet still serve meals that are delicious, attractive and within their budget.

No matter what your style, whether you're an experienced cook or just a beginner in the kitchen, **Budget Cooking** ❖ *Elegant Dining* will help you to serve delicious, attractive meals at reasonable prices and enjoy yourself while you're doing it!

Chapter One
KEYS TO BUDGETING

The three key ingredients to budgeting without sacrificing taste or quality are planning, flexibility and creativity. Let's take a look at each one, in some detail.

Planning

Proper planning can make a big difference to your budget. It can save you money at the supermarket, help you serve more interesting meals, and avoid wasting food. Here are some tips to help you plan and ease the pressure on your budget:

1. Check your local newspaper's weekly food section to see what is in season and on sale. Create a meal plan around those items. (See Menu Planning.)
2. Think about your week and your needs. Will you have a lot of company? Will you be rushed and need quick meals? Or will this be a week when you'll have time to try out a complicated new recipe?
3. Glance through the cookbook, choose the recipes you want to prepare and make a menu plan for the week.
4. Make a list of all the ingredients you'll need for making the recipes you've chosen.
5. With your meal plan and list of ingredients in front of you, make a shopping list.
6. Prepare your shopping list according to the store layout and write down the

items in the order they are laid out in the store. If you're not familiar with the store layout, at least list similar items together.

7. Eat a snack before you go to the store. It's been proven that if you shop when you're hungry, you'll overbuy, purchasing more snacks and other unnecessary items.

8. Buy *only* the items on your list, unless there are unadvertised store specials of items that you will need later.

9. Try to avoid purchasing sundries and non-food items in the grocery store, unless time is of the essence to you.

10. Try house brands or generic labels. These are often produced by famous brand companies under house labels at much lower prices.

11. Use cents-off coupons only if they're for a product you usually use. When you make out your grocery list, mark the items you have coupons for.

12. Check unit pricing (the little label on the shelf that will tell you the cost per ounce of the item). This will be a big help in deciding which brand or size is the most economical to purchase.

13. If at all possible, don't purchase convenience foods such as cake mixes or ready-made food items. You're paying a premium price for someone else to do the work for you.

14. Shop quickly. When you take your time, leisurely strolling through the aisles, you will tend to notice unfamiliar items out of curiosity and buy them on a whim.

15. Avoid busy times at the grocery store (usually 5:00 – 6:30 p.m.) and Fridays. You are more likely to make sound decisions and only purchase what you need when you're not fighting to get to a shelf or standing in line for half an hour at the check-out lane.

Some people are familiar with the prices of just about every item in every store. They always know if something is really a bargain or not. If you're one of these people, you're among the fortunate minority. I'm not, but I have friends who are, and I love to shop with them. It makes me feel like I have my own personal shopping consultant! If you don't qualify as an expert, but know someone who does, go shopping with them occasionally to learn what you can from them.

I always found I could save a fortune if I shopped without children. When the kids were with me, I would buy all sorts of extra things just because they were clamoring for them. Some people may disagree with me, but it could be cheaper to hire a baby-sitter while you grocery shop than to take the kids along. Try it both ways and see which works best for you and your family.

Buying in bulk is another great way to save. Rice, barley and beans are good examples of items that should be bought in bulk. They are not only *much* cheaper to buy in bulk but can form the basis of a meal even when the cupboard may be bare. Also, consider that the more you buy at one time, the more you save, because it means fewer trips to the store.

It may be worthwhile to become a member of one of the "no-frills" warehouse supermarkets, especially if you have a large family, a place to store the items, and available cash. These stores are usually cash-and-carry outlets.

However, a word of caution is in order here. Be careful when shopping in these stores. You will be tempted to buy items you don't really need because they are such a good deal. If you only serve pancakes six times a year, it is unwise to buy a six-pack of large-size pancake syrup just because the price is so good!

Flexibility

Flexibility is the second important aspect of budgeting. You should be flexible enough while shopping or planning your menus to take advantage of sales or seasonal items.

1. In spite of the fact that America is fortunate enough to have just about everything available all year round, it is nevertheless true that prices reflect seasonal changes. Take advantage of low prices when foods are in season. They'll be fresher and healthier, too.

2. If asparagus is a favorite, plan to use it often in the spring, when it's plentiful and inexpensive. If you're so inclined, you can even freeze some for later use during the year. If you're budget-conscious, don't even *think* about asparagus during the off season (unless you've just won a lottery!).

3. If you have company coming for dinner and have planned to make brisket and then, when you shop, you find turkey on sale, be flexible enough to switch your main course from brisket to turkey.

4. If you're just dying to try the Tomato-Basil Salad this week and the price of tomatoes has skyrocketed because of a frost or flood somewhere, be flexible (and

patient) enough to wait until the price of tomatoes comes down. Instead, make a salad using other, more reasonably priced ingredients.

Creativity

Don't feel that you have to break your budget just because friends are coming over for dinner. Be creative! Make it fun.

I once served hot dogs and baked beans for a dinner party. I called it a "Hobo Dinner" and cut out place mats from the Sunday comic section, used inexpensive paper plates, plastic cutlery and served the baked beans out of the can. The dinner was a great hit!

Another aspect of creativity is knowing how to use mistakes. And we all make mistakes! I always teach my students that unless your dish comes out a total disaster, just cover your mistake as best you can and act as though that's what you had in mind all along.

If your cake falls apart coming out of the pan, don't throw it away. Simply put it in your prettiest glass bowl, sprinkle the pieces with liqueur, dab some jam and chocolate mousse or whipped cream on it, and serve it with a smile. (No one will ever know about your disasters unless you tell them!)

What about those times when: "Five extra people are coming for dinner! What do I do now?" It all depends on what you had planned. If it's a matter of chicken soup, it's simple to add a little water and some powdered bouillon. However, that doesn't work so well when all you have is one chicken and you can't get out to the store.

Here are some creative suggestions for ways to stretch a meal:

1. Serve an appetizer. A combination of items such as pickles, olives, canned tehina, egg salad, and tuna salad with crackers can go a long way toward filling hungry stomachs.

2. Serve soup. Many soups, and especially thick ones, are very filling.

3. Serve the salad as a separate course. You can "jazz it up" a bit by adding croutons, which you can make from your leftover bread.

4. Add side dishes such as rice or pasta.

5. Add some cooked Rotini (corkscrew pasta) to your vegetable (i.e., string beans) and sprinkle with garlic salt and olive oil.

6. Make a gelatin mold with canned fruit salad in it.

Budgeting is the smart way to cook. You'll create delicious, exciting meals — sure to please — while still saving money. Using the tips in this book, plus some common sense and moderation, budgeting will become second nature to you. You'll gain some great ideas on how to save money and learn to prepare some fabulous new dishes, too!

❖❖❖

Chapter Two
ELEGANT DINING

Elegant dining does not necessarily mean formal dining. It simply means giving thought and effort to producing well-balanced meals presented attractively. It can also mean serving hamburgers and hot dogs in a fun, creative way.

My cousin, Andy Steinman, who graduated from the Cordon Bleu in London, said the largest segment of time was spent on food presentation. You can take the simplest dish and make it very special, or conversely, you can take the most special dish and make it very ordinary by the way you present it.

It doesn't take much effort or expense. Remember to take the time to arrange the food attractively on a dish or platter and add a bit of garnish.

You may be serving "only family", but even children will notice and appreciate it. You may also be surprised at the difference in children's behavior when the table is set nicely and the food looks pretty.

Some hints to make your meals more elegant:

1. If you are in the market for a new set of dishes, consider a set of simple, white dishes. They can dress up a formal dinner party or become casual or ethnic, depending on the tablecloths and napkins you use.

    With solid white, or any other solid color dishes you can:

    a) Use a black tablecloth and napkins, and you have the perfect setting for an elegant formal dinner party.

    b) Use a floral flat sheet as a tablecloth to create a beautiful spring or fall casual, but elegant dinner.

c) If you have a serape or unusual piece of fabric, drape it across a white tablecloth to create an ethnic look.

2. Try using cloth napkins. They add to the atmosphere of the meal and are very economical if you use synthetic fabrics that don't require ironing. Rather than using matched sets of cloth napkins, I like to use different colors or prints. They can usually be found on sale.

3. Use natural garnishes (fruit, vegetables) to beautify your platters of food. They don't have to be elaborate. Sometimes the simplest garnishes are the best...a few cherry tomatoes, a bunch of fresh herbs, perhaps a flower from your garden.

4. A slice or two of fresh lemon in your pitcher of water adds a great deal of elegance to your table.

5. Use fresh ingredients, especially garlic, ginger, ground pepper, herbs, lemons and mushrooms.

6. Stemware glasses, which are not necessarily costly, add a great deal to any table.

7. Candied flowers, sold in gourmet shops, make lively decorations for cakes or desserts. They keep for several months if stored in a tightly covered container. If you prefer to make these elegant decoration yourself, here's what to do:

    a) Use freshly picked unsprayed violets with stems attached (baby roses, or any other small, edible flower will do).

    b) Holding each violet by its stem, dip blossom into 1 beaten egg white, letting excess drain off.

    c) Dip into sugar.

    d) Let dry on wire rack. After flowers are thoroughly dried, break off and discard stem.

8. If you're serving a buffet, make sure that all the foods served are bite-sized. There is nothing less elegant or more awkward than trying to eat a plate full of food balanced on your lap. All buffet food should be prepared to enable a guest to eat with only a fork.

❖❖❖

Chapter Three
HOW TO USE LEFTOVERS

Unfortunately, the word "leftover" seems to have a bad connotation for many people. They think in terms of stale food and unappetizing meals — but this needn't be the case. Skillful use of leftovers is one of the biggest aids to budgeting. There are many creative ways to use leftovers. In fact, when you cook, try to keep in mind options for using them.

Don't let your leftovers sit in the refrigerator until they grow mold and have to be thrown out. Use them wisely, but also plan to use them in a variety of ways so your meals don't get monotonous.

If you serve a tuna dish for dinner one night, send the children off to school with tuna sandwiches the next day. If you serve corn for dinner, use the leftovers in a corn chowder or corn souffle a day or two later instead of serving corn two or three nights in a row.

Using leftovers doesn't have to be an exact science, either. You just need a little creativity. For example, if a casserole or quiche recipe calls for 2 cups of green beans and you happen to have $1/2$ cup of green beans and $1^1/_2$ cups of cooked carrots left over in your refrigerator, combine the vegetables to get the amount called for in the recipe.

Here are some "tried-and-true" suggestions for dealing with leftovers:

1. Keep a container in your refrigerator or freezer for vegetable leftovers. Just put them all together in the same container: a half cup of green beans, a few tablespoons of corn, some tomato. You can also save the water that the vegetables were cooked in — that's where all the nutrients are. Every few days, or when the container is full, take out the container and you have the makings of a delicious vegetable soup. Try Ten-Layer Vegetable Soup, substituting your leftover vegetables for the vegetables and broth called for in the recipe. Leftover cooked pasta or grains (barley, etc.), can be added to the soup just before

serving. However, if you let these vegetables sit too long they'll become mushy and you'll have a soup that your family will refuse to eat.

2. Save beef bones and chicken or turkey carcasses to make soup and/or stews. Use them in a recipe that calls for them specifically; or, you can cook the bones and make a broth to use as a base for other soups. The best way to do this is to cook the bones in water to cover and add a tablespoon of vinegar. This draws the calcium from the bones and increases the nutritional value of the broth. If you don't use the broth immediately, freeze it for later use.

3. At least once a week go through your refrigerator and freezer to see what leftovers need to be used up before they rot. Leftovers that sit in the freezer for long periods of time get freezer burn and lose their flavor.

4. Chinese dishes are an excellent way to use leftover meat. Shred the cooked meat, stir fry with some onions and garlic and add any leftover vegetables you have as long as they're still pretty crisp.
   If you don't have any leftover vegetables, first stir-fry some sliced onions, carrots, garlic, and whatever fresh vegetables you have on hand. Then add the meat, a tablespoon or two of soy sauce, $1/2$ teaspoon of fresh or powdered ginger and stir-fry just long enough to heat through.

5. Leftover mashed potatoes can be used as a topping for a pot pie. Or, add a beaten egg or two (depending on the amount of mashed potatoes), 1 teaspoon baking powder, salt to taste, and make potato pancakes. You can also try making potato soup from the leftovers. Instead of the amount of raw potatoes called for in the recipe, simply substitute an equal amount of cooked mashed potatoes and reduce the cooking time.

6. Before cheese gets moldy, save the odd bits in a bag in the freezer for later use in lasagnas and other casseroles.

7. Serve leftover gravy and meat bits, from a roast, over leftover mashed potatoes or cooked noodles.

8. Save leftover bread in the freezer. You can use it to make sweet dessert bread puddings, croutons, seasoned bread crumbs, or stuffing.
   Another possibility is to make French toast and store it in the freezer. This makes an excellent and quick breakfast for kids. Simply remove from the freezer and heat in the microwave or toaster oven.

You can get started using leftovers creatively with the following recipes. They are all excellent budget stretchers.

❖ To use up leftover brisket, pot roast or roast beef, try:

Barbecued Beef	139
Stew Pot Beef	140
"Glop" Salad	156
Cholent I	135
Cholent II	136

❖ To use up leftover poultry, try:

Lemon-Garlic Chicken	155
"Glop" Salad	156
Quick Chicken Pot Pie	154
Barbecued Chicken	153

Note: Some of these recipes call for cooked chicken or turkey. In others, the leftover meat can just be reheated with the sauce called for in the recipe.

❖ To use up leftover vegetables, try:

Ten-Layer Vegetable Soup	91
Passover Vegetable Kugel	222

Pot Pie	154
Middle-Eastern Rice Salad	101

❖ More suggestions for leftover vegetables:
Sprinkle them with toasted sesame seeds or chopped toasted nuts.
Sprinkle $1/2$ cup seasoned bread crumbs mixed with 2 tablespoons melted margarine over vegetables and heat.

❖ To use up leftover breads and/or challah, try:

Cheese Casserole	131
Seasoned Bread Crumbs	75
Berry Bread Pudding	190

❖ To use up leftover fish, try:

Leftover Fish Casserole	114
Fish Mousse	50

With a little practice, you'll come up with plenty of your own creative ideas to use your leftovers.

❖❖❖

Chapter Four
MENU PLANNING

Menu planning is another important aspect of budgeting, and, just like budgeting, it is an acquired skill. Many of my cooking students have told me that the most difficult thing about cooking is deciding what to cook and how to plan the menu.

My advice is to make it easy and write down your menus in a notebook or calendar. Use the food section of the newspaper to see what is on sale and in season and plan your meals around those items. Utilizing produce when it is in season will help your budget as well as vary your menus naturally. Plan your menus at least a week in advance, further ahead if possible.

Prepare your grocery list at the same time you plan your menus. List every single ingredient you will need for each meal, then check through your pantry and refrigerator and cross off the items you already have. If such detailed planning of every course of every meal is just beyond you, try to at least plan your main courses.

Keep your family's schedule in mind. On days that will be particularly busy, plan something simple with quick clean-up. Save more complicated dishes for days when you'll have more time for them.

When planning a menu consider not only the free time you have available, but also the time of the year. First, seasonal foods are always freshest and most economical (i.e., lush strawberries, peaches and asparagus in the springtime; citrus fruit and crisp apples and pears in the fall). Also, while heavier, steamy soup may be appealing and comforting in the winter, you'll want cool, light, crisp salads for the summer.

When I planned my first Passover Seder I was very nervous about doing everything "just so." I decided to leave nothing to chance: in addition to my shopping and cooking lists, my refrigerator door held a detailed list of the menu, what silverware and serving pieces were to be used for each course, what should be on the table and what should be removed from the table at each part of the meal, and when to refill the wine and water glasses. I did carry it to an extreme and now I can laugh about it, but at the time it was very comforting to have all those lists to refer to.

Consider using a single meat for more than one meal, but not necessarily for two days in a row. For example, serve pot roast one night and freeze the remainder to make barbecued beef or stir-fried beef a few nights later. On the other hand, if your family loves brisket or roast chicken and prefers eating it a second time around instead of in a different dish made from the leftovers, by all means serve it that way. The point is to serve what pleases you and your family. Just remember that even steak can get boring after you've had it three nights in a row!

Plan your meals to include interesting combinations of foods with different colors and textures. It is said that we feast first with our eyes and then with our stomachs. Meals where all the food is the same color (chicken, cauliflower, and rice or mashed potatoes) appear boring and unappetizing. If you are serving chicken as a main course, plan to also serve green beans, glazed carrots, and a colorful salad with red tomatoes and purple cabbage.

Keep an inventory of what you have in the freezer and mark items clearly (with the date) so you can use them up before they get relegated to the garbage. Even in the freezer, food doesn't last forever. If you have a separate freezer, keep all the chicken and meat items on one shelf, vegetables on another, desserts on still another. Keep a sheet of lined paper on the door of the freezer and when you put something in the freezer, add it to the list. When you remove an item, cross it off the list. Even if your list isn't consistently updated or completely accurate, this system will make it much easier for you to keep track of what you have in the freezer. No more standing in front of the freezer with the door open checking to see what you have and trying to figure out what to cook.

While detailed lists for every meal, with plans to use up every bit of leftover food, would be nice, this system doesn't work for everyone. If it all seems like more than you can cope with, don't worry. Remember, even a little planning is better than none at all. The more you practice these techniques, the sooner you'll discover how easy it is to save money...and eat well too.

❖❖❖

Chapter Five
JEWISH HOLIDAYS AND LIFE CYCLE EVENTS

No kosher cookbook would be complete without a section on Jewish Holidays and Life Cycle Events because both they and the foods associated with them are such an important part of our lives.

Guided by the memories and traditions of Judaism, it lies within the power of every Jew with just a little effort and with lots of love and enthusiasm to transform whatever house they may occupy into a beautiful Jewish home. The lessons and memories associated with the holidays become deeply impressed upon a child's mind. The ceremonies around the family table, and traditional Jewish foods are as important to children as what they learn in school. The Jewish mother and father are the true teachers of our children and the home plays a great part in the traditions of Judaism.

Shabbat

God created the world in six days, and on the seventh day, Shabbat, He rested. That's why Shabbat has become a day of rest for the Jewish people since Biblical times. Cooking is not permitted on Shabbat, so food is prepared before Shabbat. Yet, the richness and diversity of the Shabbat table, and the warmth of the Shabbat itself, more than make up for some of the cold food served at the Shabbat meal.

The famous story of *Yosef Mokir Shabbat*, Joseph who loved the Shabbat, describes how one poor man saved up money each week so he could buy the best fish for Shabbat, and the magnificent reward he received for doing so.

However, while Jews put out their finest cutlery and dishes on Shabbat, you don't have to spend your last dollar to prepare wonderful Shabbat meals. Sitting with family and friends, and singing Shabbat songs, can sometimes transform a simple meat loaf into an elegant and sumptuous meal.

Best of all, because I can't cook on Shabbat, I get to appreciate those times when I can.

Suggested Menus

#1

Gefilte Fish with horseradish
Chicken Soup
Beverly's Brisket
Broccoli Kugel
Layered Salad
Carrot Cake
with Parve Vanilla Ice Cream

#2

Halibut Salad
Baked Chicken Epstein
Amy's Potato Kugel
Glazed Baby Carrots
Tossed Green Salad
Banana Split Dessert

Melave Malka

There is a tradition to eat a light meal on Saturday night, after the Shabbat is over, in honor of the Shabbat Queen with whom we can hardly bear to part. You can prepare a simple, light meal or try my favorite plan. I like to call friends, when Shabbat is over, and tell them to bring whatever leftovers they have and come for a Melave Malka. Everyone seems to delight in this type of spur-of-the-moment, casual evening, and it's a fun and inexpensive way to entertain.

Suggested Menus

#1	#2
Easy Lasagna Squares	Hummus
Green Salad	Tehina
Tuna Salad	Turkish Salad
Garlic Bread	Mediterranean Salad
Cranberry Ice	Cheese Casserole
	Strawberries in Orange Juice

Rosh Hashana

Rosh Hashana is the anniversary of the creation of the world. It is a time of contemplation and introspection, and, as with all Jewish holidays, also a time of family gathering and togetherness.

Before the main meal is served, the traditional table is covered with foods representing optimism and hope for a good and sweet new year. Each food has its individual blessing and symbolism: apples dipped in honey for a good and sweet year; gourds, for our merits to be proclaimed before God; pomegranates, for our merits to increase like the seeds; fish, so that we may be fruitful and multiply like the fish. I like to serve as many of these symbolic foods as possible. Some people prefer to choose only one or two.

Suggested Menus

#1

Gefilte Fish

Chicken Marengo

Israeli Rice

Glazed Baby Carrots

Broccoli Kugel

French Apple Pie

#2

Ten-Layer Vegetable Soup

Baked Nile Perch

Vegetable Cheese Pie

Layered Salad

Carrot Cake

Sukkot

Sukkot, the Festival of Booths, is a festival of rejoicing and fun. It is celebrated for seven days, beginning the 15th day of Tishrei in the Jewish calendar, and commemorates the fact that the Jews leaving Egypt had to live in flimsy booths in the desert, depending entirely on God to protect them from the elements. It is also the season of the ingathering of the harvest.

All meals are eaten in the sukkah and as much time as possible is spent there. Many Jews sleep in their sukkah for the entire week.

Because Sukkot also symbolizes the richness of the harvest, many vegetables are served, especially stuffed ones, such as Stuffed Cabbage or Stuffed Eggplant and Strudels.

Suggested Menus

#1	#2
Stuffed Cabbage	Fresh Vegetable Platter
Roast Turkey with Bread Stuffing	Sweet and Sour Pot Roast
Tsimmes	Amy's Potato Kugel
Applesauce	Tomato-Basil Salad
Shredded Lettuce with Tomato Salad	French Apple Pie
Jelly Roll or Strudel	

Shmini Atzeret and Simchat Torah

Shmini Atzeret is celebrated the day after Sukkot, and symbolizes our reluctance to leave the sukkah and God's desire to have us stay with Him another day. The next day is Simchat Torah which is literally a day of rejoicing with the Torah. In the synagogue, Jews dance and sing, carrying the Torah scrolls, while children join in waving flags. At the end of the festivities, the last section of the Torah is read and the first section of Genesis is read immediately thereafter.

Because services often run late, both on Simchat Torah evening and in the morning, I find it easiest to make a simple meal that can be eaten whenever everyone straggles in from synagogue.

Suggested Menus

#1
Cream of Cauliflower Soup
Baked Chicken Epstein
String Beans
Celery & Carrot Sticks
Middle Eastern Rice Salad
Mandel Bread

#2
Avocado Appetizer
"Glop" Salad
Tomato-Basil Salad
Kasha Salad
Pineapple Split Cake

Hanukkah

Hanukkah commemorates the Maccabees' victory over the Greeks and the rededication of the Holy Temple in Jerusalem. Candles are lit by members of the family in the windows of the home, Hanukkah songs are sung, and dreidel and other games are played. Because one day's supply of oil lasted for eight days at the rededication of the Holy Temple, it is traditional to eat foods cooked in oil. Potato latkes and *sufganiyot* (yeast-raised jelly donuts) are two of the most traditional Hanukkah foods.

Hanukkah is an inexpensive time to entertain. The foods are simple. I often invite friends and neighbors for an evening consisting of a light meal of potato latkes, served with applesauce and sour cream. One friend of mine has an annual Hanukkah party and serves potato latkes, fruit salad and her Hungarian mother-in-law's most amazing sufganiyot, accompanied by her Russian grandmother's home-made jams for dipping.

Suggested Menu

Lentil Soup

Potato Latkes

Eggplant Fritters

Applesauce and/or Sour Cream

Pan-Fried Fish

Green Salad

Sufganiyot

Fresh Fruit Salad

Purim

In celebration of the Jews' delivery from the evil Haman in ancient Persia, Jews read the Book of Esther in the synagogue. Charity is given to the poor, and *mishloach manot* (gifts of food), are delivered to friends. A festive meal is eaten in the afternoon on the day of the holiday. It is a joyous holiday and children from ages 1 to 120 dress in costumes and masks.

Purim is an easy time to get carried away, buying expensive mishloach manot baskets and food items to send to friends. With a little creativity, it doesn't have to be an expensive holiday.

There are many creative, inexpensive and thoughtful mishloach manot ideas. Try using masks as baskets for your mishloach manot. My daughter sends a lemon and a peppermint candy stick together with illustrated instructions on how to put the two together and enjoy the peppermint lemonade!

Pre-Purim is also a great time to spend with your children making *Hamantashen*, a traditional Purim treat. It is a perfect afternoon's entertainment and the stuff that tomorrow's memories are made of.

Suggested Menu

Curried Carrot Soup
Barbecued Beef
Applesauce Loaf
Broccoli Kugel
Layered Salad
Hamantashen
Reverse Hamantashen

Passover

The *Haggadah*, the story of Passover, reminds every Jew to feel as if he or she, personally, had been saved from slavery and taken out of Egypt. The ritual symbols and ceremonies associated with the traditional *Seder*, or Passover meal, remind us of the bitter experience of oppression and slavery, and of the joy of freedom. The entire holiday is full of potentially fun, exciting and involving activities for the kids. At the Seder, the Hagaddah is read to convey the Passover story to our children.

Because of the exacting requirements for keeping kosher during Passover and the large number of holiday meals, it is the most difficult time to stay on a budget. In fact, it's almost impossible! The most you can hope for is to try and keep things within reason. My best suggestion is stick to fresh fruits and vegetables as much as possible.

If Kosher-for-Passover orange juice is exorbitant, for one week squeeze fresh oranges or other fruits yourself. I never purchase mayonnaise and salad dressings, especially during Passover.

Kosher-for-Passover candies are especially expensive. Figure out the price per ounce of these goodies and it will knock your socks off! Yet most of us, who rarely buy candy during the rest of the year, seem to feel the need to stock up on this luxury item during Passover. If you can resist the temptation, stay away from the candies, both for budgetary and dietary reasons.

Because Passover occurs in the spring, fresh fruits and vegetables are generally plentiful and inexpensive. It's very easy to plan your menus around these foods and it's a great way to economize during Passover. (If you're an asparagus lover, this is definitely the time to buy and serve mounds of this vegetable which is so high-priced the remainder of the year.)

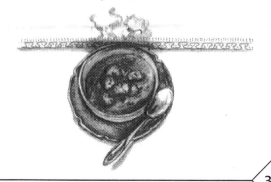

When planning your Seder menu, keep in mind that most traditional Jews eat specified amounts of *matzo, carpas, haroset,* etc., during the Seder itself. When its time for the festive meal, everyone is usually so full that it's difficult to eat a huge meal and stay awake for the remainder of the Seder.

Suggested Menus

#1	#2
Gefilte Fish with Horseradish	*A lighter Seder menu:*
Chicken Soup with Matzo Balls	Gefilte Fish with Horseradish
Beverly's Brisket	Chicken Soup with Matzo Balls
Matzo Kugel	Baked Chicken with Mushrooms
Spiced Carrots	Mixed Green Salad
Fresh Garden Asparagus	Fresh Fruit Salad
Layered Salad	
Strawberries in Orange Juice	

Shavuot

Shavuot arrives seven weeks after Passover and celebrates the giving of the Torah by God to the Jewish nation on Mount Sinai. Milk and honey have always symbolized the richness of Torah and the Land of Israel, and thus it is customary to eat dairy foods on Shavuot.

Cheesecake is one of the foods that has become synonymous with Shavuot. I also like to use this holiday as an opportunity to try new dairy recipes.

Suggested Menu

Cold Strawberry Soup
Salmon Florentine Pie
Blintz Casserole with Blueberry or Cherry Pie Filling
Marinated Vegetables
Lettuce, Tomato and Cucumber Salad
Arlene's Cheesecake

Shalom Zachor (Welcoming a newborn boy)

On the first Friday night after a son is born, even if mother and baby are still in the hospital, friends gather at the home of the newborn after Shabbat dinner. The father greets the guests and there is much singing and well-wishing.

It is traditional to serve chick peas, with simple sweets and drinks. It is not necessary to serve a lavish spread — most people will have just come from their Shabbat dinner.

Brit Milah (Circumcision of a baby boy)

If you are fortunate enough to have a home or synagogue big enough to hold a Brit Milah, it need not be an extravagant and expensive event. Most circumcisions are held in the morning, right after services because this mitzvah is supposed to be carried out as early as possible on the eighth day.

Many people will come for the ceremony, eat a quick bite and go on to work or their daily obligations. It is a good idea to have some drinks and cakes for those who cannot stay for the meal.

Suggested Menus

#1	#2
Cold Cut Platter	Miniature Bagels with
Pickles and Olives	Cream Cheese & Lox Spread
Cole Slaw	Butter / Jam
Potato Salad	Herring
Mediterranean Salad	Eggs with Caviar
Relish Tray	Tuna Salad
Assorted Breads	Vegetable Cheese Pie
Fresh Seasonal Fruit Salad	Carrot and Cucumber Sticks
Assorted Sweets	Assorted Sweets

Pidyon Haben (Redemption of the firstborn son)

When a first-born baby boy is not the son of a Kohen or Levi (a descendant of the priestly class), a *Pidyon Haben* ceremony is held on the 30th day after his birth. This is a biblical ritual by which the baby is redeemed from a Kohen for five silver coins. Afterwards a meal is served. The menu can be the same as that for a Brit Milah.

Bar/Bat Mitzvah

Upon reaching the designated age (12 years for a girl, 13 for a boy), the Jewish child is surrounded by family and friends to celebrate his/her entrance into Jewish adulthood.

It is traditional to have a party to celebrate a boy's first *aliyah* to the Torah, and his taking on the obligations of a Jewish adult. It has also become popular for girls to celebrate reaching this crucial age too.

It is important to keep in mind the auspiciousness of the occasion when planning the party. In this era of casual entertaining, it can be fun and appropriate to have a home celebration. It is a wonderful time for extended families to gather and renew the ties that bind. It is also a good time to have all your friends pitch in and help!

Suggested Menus

#1	#2
Dairy Buffet:	*Meat Buffet:*
Fresh Mushroom Soup	Fresh Cut-up Vegetables and Dip
Salad Bar (bowls of lettuce,	Chicken Superlative
shredded carrots, sliced cucumbers,	Sweet and Sour Meatballs
canned corn, cherry tomatoes,	Lemon Vegetables
green pepper strips, chopped hard	Rice
cooked eggs, croutons)	Marinated Vegetables
French Dressing	Mediterranean Salad
Vinaigrette Dressing	Assorted Desserts
Oriental Dressing	Bar/Bat Mitzvah Cake
Vegetable Quiche	
Easy Lasagna Squares	
Excellent Fish	
Assorted Breads with Herb Butter	
Ice Cream Bar (vanilla and	
chocolate ice cream	
with hot fudge sauce,	
cherry pie filling, and caramel sauce)	

Hanukkat Habayit (House warming)

When a Jew moves into a new house, he is obligated to attach a mezuzah the doorposts of his home. It is not necessary to make a special occasion of this, but many people take the opportunity to celebrate and invite friends and neighbors to their new home. You can serve an assortment of desserts and drinks, or choose a suggested meal from Menu Planning, if you wish.

Shevah Brachot (Seven Blessings)

When a Jewish couple marries, they are traditionally the center of attention not only at their wedding, but for seven days of celebration afterward. Rather than immediately leaving for a honeymoon, they are feted for a week with parties, or dinners, held in their honor. These festive meals celebrate the couple's new status as husband and wife.

Suggested Menus

#1	#2
Fresh Cut Vegetables and Dip	Quick 'n' Easy Bean Soup
Chicken Drumstick Crown	Marinated Vegetables
Spiced Orange Rice	Meatloaf in Puff Pastry
Broccoli Kugel	Garlic Bread or Bubble Bread
Layered Salad	Mixed Green Salad
Dacquoise au Chocolat	Roulade

Seudat Havrah (Meal of Consolation)

When Jewish mourners return from the cemetery, friends, neighbors, or in some instances a committee from the synagogue, bring a meal to the home where they are sitting *Shiva*, the seven-day mourning period.

The consolation meal is not an elaborate one. The mourners are generally not in a mood to eat. A light dairy meal is usually served. The only traditional food served at this meal is hard-boiled eggs, a symbol of the life cycle.

Suggested Menu

Hard-boiled Eggs
Tuna Fish Salad
Potato Cheese Kugel
Farmer's Casserole
Mixed Green Salad
Mandel Bread

❖❖❖

Chapter Six
APPETIZERS

Whether it's called *forspeis*, hors d'oeuvres, or first course, appetizers make a meal special. They can also be a boon to the budget.

If you are serving an expensive roast, try serving an appetizer consisting of a lettuce-lined plate with sliced hard-boiled eggs garnished with a dollop of mustard-mayonnaise and a cherry tomato or olive. This is a lovely, simple and inexpensive way to dress up a meal.

If you want the appetizer to be a filling one, try something like the recipe for Mushrooms and Onions on Couscous.

Some of the appetizers in this section, such as Sweet and Sour Meatballs, and Fish Mousse, can also be served as a main course.

Stuffed Vegetable Medley

❖ **Notes** ❖

Can be prepared up to three days ahead and refrigerated.

❖❖❖

6	medium zucchini	12	eggs, beaten
6	yellow crookneck squash	3	cups very fine dry bread crumbs
2	medium red or Spanish onions	$3/4$	teaspoon marjoram, crumbled
6	firm medium tomatoes	$1/2$	teaspoon salt or to taste
6	medium green peppers		A dash of fresh ground pepper
7	tablespoons olive oil		Fresh parsley, minced
$1/2$	onion, finely chopped		

❖❖❖

1. Parboil zucchini and yellow squash in large amount of salted water until *just* tender.
2. Remove from pot with slotted spoon and drain well. Rinse under cold running water and drain again (this stops the cooking process).
3. Add onions to same water and parboil until tender. Drain well, rinse under cold running water and drain again.
4. Cut tomatoes in half and scoop out pulp, leaving $1/4$-inch shell (do not pierce skin). Set pulp aside.
5. Cut peppers in half and remove seeds.
6. Halve zucchini and yellow squash horizontally and scoop out pulp, leaving $1/4$-inch shell.
7. Halve onions from root to top; remove centers, leaving a thin shell.
8. Heat 5 tablespoons of the olive oil in a large skillet. Add finely chopped onion and saute until lightly golden.

(Recipe continued...)

Stuffed Vegetable Medley... *(Recipe continued...)*

9. Chop tomato, zucchini and yellow squash pulp along with the onion centers. Add to skillet and cook 10 minutes, stirring frequently.
10. Transfer mixture to a large bowl and let cool.
11. Preheat oven to 325°.
12. Generously oil large shallow baking dish.
13. Add eggs, breadcrumbs, marjoram, salt, and pepper to vegetable mixture and blend thoroughly.
14. Taste and adjust seasoning (it should be very highly seasoned).
15. Arrange vegetable shells in single layer in baking dish so sides do not touch.
16. Fill shells with breadcrumb mixture.
17. Bake until filling is set, about 15 – 20 minutes.
18. Drizzle with olive oil and sprinkle with parsley.
19. Broil until filling is lightly golden. Let cool in pan.

❖ **Notes** ❖

Melon and Smoked Turkey

Meat
6 servings

Purchase the smoked turkey at the deli counter and ask them to slice it paper thin.

❖❖❖

3   large ripe cantaloupes or other
       melon
¹/₂ pound smoked turkey, sliced
       very thin
    Lemon wedges for garnish

❖❖❖

1. Cut melon into thin slices: remove rind.
2. Wrap each piece of melon in a slice of smoked turkey.
3. Place 3 – 4 slices of wrapped melon on each plate.
4. Garnish with lemon wedges.

Avocado Appetizer

❖ **Notes** ❖

A great appetizer to serve when avocados are in season and inexpensive. May also be used as a dip with corn chips.

❖❖❖

3   **very ripe avocados**
3   **hard-boiled eggs**
    Juice of ¹/₂ lemon
1   **teaspoon Worcestershire sauce**
¹/₈ **teaspoon garlic salt**
    **Approximately 3 tablespoons
        mayonnaise**
    **A dash of Tabasco or hot
        pepper sauce (optional)**
    Lettuce leaves
    Olive oil

❖❖❖

1. Mash eggs and avocados.
2. Add lemon juice, Worcestershire sauce, garlic salt and enough mayonnaise to bind it together.
3. Add Tabasco sauce if desired.
4. Serve on a bed of lettuce. Decorate with tomato wedges and sprinkle with a drop or two of olive oil and lemon juice.

❖ Some brands of Worcestershire sauce are not parve.

Baked Bologna

Meat
6-8 servings

Simple to make and watch it disappear! If you do have leftovers, they make great sandwiches.

❖❖❖

1	**3-pound whole bologna**
	Mustard

❖❖❖

1. Score bologna with a sharp knife lengthwise every 2 inches.
2. Place bologna on a rack over a baking pan and bake 3 hours in a 250° oven or until outside is crisp; or it may be cooked on a grill.
3. Slice, and spread with mustard, and serve with crackers or party rye bread, as an hors d'oeuvre.
4. If served as a first course, serve sliced on a bed of lettuce.

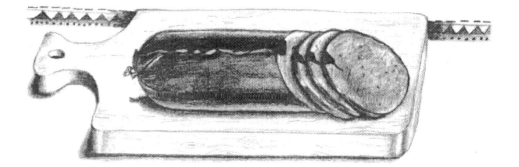

❖ Salami may be substituted for bologna.

Marinated Vegetables

Parve
16 servings

Simple, delicious and it keeps well in the refrigerator.

❖❖❖

1	can peas, drained	1	cup oil
1	can corn, drained	$^1/_2$	cup sugar
1	cup chopped celery	1	teaspoon pepper
1	can beans, drained	$^3/_4$	cup vinegar
1	cup chopped onions	1	teaspoon salt
1	cup chopped green pepper	1	small jar capers, drained

❖❖❖

Mix and enjoy.

❖ Any fresh, frozen or canned vegetables may be substituted.

Eggs with Caviar

Dairy
12 servings

❖ **Notes** ❖

This is definitely a party dish. It looks lovely served in a glass bowl.

❖❖❖

12	eggs, hard-boiled
3	green onions, finely chopped
	Approximately $3/4$ cup mayonnaise
1	teaspoon salt, or to taste
$1/4$	teaspoon pepper, or to taste
1	cup sour cream
1	$3^1/2$ ounce jar kosher caviar, red or black

❖❖❖

1. Peel and chop cooked eggs.
2. Add green onions and enough mayonnaise to hold mixture together.
3. Season with salt and pepper.
4. Place in a shallow ceramic or glass bowl and top with sour cream.
5. Shortly before serving, cover with caviar. Serve with party rye bread or crackers.

Eggplant Fritters

Parve
6 servings

❖❖❖

2   cups cooked mashed eggplant
1 ¹/₂ cups cooked white rice
1   cup fine bread crumbs
¹/₃ cup finely chopped onion
2   eggs, well beaten
1   teaspoon salt, or to taste
¹/₄ teaspoon pepper, or to taste
     A dash of red pepper sauce
     Oil

❖❖❖

1. Combine all ingredients except oil.
2. Heat ¹/₂-inch oil in a large skillet over medium heat.
3. Drop mixture by tablespoons into oil and fry until golden brown, turning once.
4. Drain on paper towels. Serve hot.

❖ Fritters can be frozen after frying and reheated in a 350° oven for 10 minutes.

Fish Mousse

❖ **Notes** ❖

This recipe is an elegant way to use up a modest amount of leftover fish. The mousse has a crunchy, interesting texture.

❖❖❖

¹/₂	cup cold water
2	teaspoons kosher gelatin
³/₄	cup mayonnaise
1	cup leftover fish, flaked
¹/₂	cup minced celery
¹/₂	cup peeled, seeded, minced cucumber
1¹/₂	tablespoons chopped fresh dill
2–3	teaspoons lemon juice
³/₄	teaspoon kosher salt
	A dash freshly ground pepper

❖❖❖

1. Place the water in a small saucepan. Sprinkle the gelatin over the water to soak.
2. Place the pan over low heat and stir until the gelatin is dissolved.
3. Let cool.
4. When cool, stir the gelatin into the mayonnaise.
5. Add remaining ingredients and mix well.
6. Season to taste.
7. Pour mixture into an oiled 3 – 4 cup mold. Chill until set, about 3 hours.
8. Unmold and slice.
9. Serve with Cucumber Mint Sauce (see opposite page).

Cucumber Mint Sauce

Parve
1 cup

❖ **Notes** ❖

❖❖❖

1   **cup mayonnaise**
¹/₂ **cup peeled, seeded, minced
      cucumbers**
1   **tablespoon chopped fresh mint
      or ¹/₄ teaspoon dry mint**
¹/₂ **teaspoon minced garlic**
¹/₂ **teaspoon salt**

❖❖❖

Combine all ingredients and mix well.

Halibut Salad

❖ Notes ❖

❖❖❖

2	pounds fillet of halibut (or any other similar fish fillet)
1	lemon, sliced
1	small onion, sliced
$^1/_4$	teaspoon allspice
1	bay leaf
1	teaspoon salt
$^1/_2$	teaspoon pepper
3	hard-boiled eggs
$^1/_2$	cup diced celery
$^1/_4$	cup chili sauce
$^1/_4$	cup mayonnaise

❖❖❖

1. Combine halibut with lemon, onion and seasonings and cook in a small amount of water until tender. May be microwaved.
2. Drain fish, cool and flake.
3. Combine remaining ingredients and add to flaked fish. Mix.
4. Correct seasonings to taste.
5. Chill thoroughly. May be molded.

Tuna Loaf

This is a delicious alternative to Gefilte Fish. It can be served either as an appetizer or main course. You will need a large piece of cheesecloth for this.

❖❖❖

1	cup bread crumbs	$^1/_4$	cup lemon juice
2	7-ounce cans tuna fish	1	teaspoon salt
2	eggs	$^1/_2$	teaspoon black pepper
1	tablespoon capers	1	large onion, peeled and sliced
$^1/_2$	cup fresh parsley, finely chopped	1	cup dry white wine, optional
			Lettuce for garnish

❖❖❖

1. Puree bread crumbs, tuna fish and eggs in food processor until smooth.
2. Remove mixture to a bowl and add capers, parsley, lemon juice, salt and pepper.
3. Wet cheesecloth, placing tuna mixture in center. Carefully shape it into a log. Fold cloth to cover and tie ends tightly with string or twist-tie and place in a soup pot.
4. Add sliced onion, wine and enough water to cover loaf by about $^1/_2$-inch.
5. Bring to a boil over high heat, then simmer covered for $^1/_2$ hour.
6. Uncover and let cool.
7. Remove tuna loaf and unwrap. Cool for $^1/_2$ hour.
8. Wrap in foil or plastic wrap and refrigerate until ready to serve.
9. Cut into $^1/_2$-inch slices and serve on a bed of lettuce.

❖ **Notes** ❖

❖ A new cloth diaper may be used instead of cheesecloth.

❖ **Notes** ❖

Tahina

Tahina is a delicious Middle Eastern staple and is becoming very popular in America. It is generally served as an appetizer with hummus, eggplant salad, Turkish salad, pickles and olives. It also makes a good dip for vegetables.

❖❖❖

1	**cup canned tahina paste**
$^1/_4$	**cup water**
$^1/_2$	**cup or more lemon juice**
4	**cloves garlic, mashed**
1	**teaspoon salt**
1	**cup finely chopped fresh parsley**
$^1/_2$	**cup finely chopped mint, (optional)**

❖❖❖

1. In a food processor or blender mix the tahina, water and lemon juice.
2. Add garlic cloves and salt. Taste the mixture for seasoning; you may want to add more water and/or lemon juice.
3. To serve, spread tehina on a flat plate and make a shallow swirl design in it with the back of a teaspoon. Drizzle olive oil over the mixture and sprinkle with finely chopped parsley and mint.

Hummus

Parve
12 servings

❖❖❖

2   **cups canned chickpeas, drained**
²/₃ **cup canned tahina paste**
¹/₂ **cup lemon juice or more**
2   **cloves garlic**
1   **teaspoon salt**
     Garnish: finely chopped parsley

❖❖❖

1. Place all the ingredients in a food processor or blender and mix until the mixture is smooth.
2. Taste for seasoning and consistency. More garlic or lemon juice may be added.
3. Store in a covered container in the refrigerator.
4. Serve garnished with parsley.

Turkish Salad

❖ **Notes** ❖

This salad is generally served as an appetizer in combination with tahina, hummus, pickles, olives and perhaps an eggplant salad. It can be made fiery, if you like, with the addition of hot red peppers or red pepper sauce.

❖❖❖

$^1/_2$ **pound (about 4) sweet red peppers**
1 **pound (about 3 medium) onions, coarsely chopped**
1 **8$^1/_2$ ounce can tomato puree**
2 **tablespoons lemon juice**
4 **tablespoons olive oil**
1 **tablespoon salt, or to taste**
1–2 **hot red peppers or $^1/_8$ teaspoon red pepper sauce, optional**

❖❖❖

1. Seed and coarsely chop sweet red peppers and place in food processor together with remaining ingredients. Blend briefly, but do not puree. It should be coarsely chopped.

2. Taste and correct seasonings, if necessary.

3. Store in a covered container in the refrigerator. Turkish salad will keep for several weeks if refrigerated.

Mushrooms & Onions on Couscous

Dairy or Parve
6 servings

This is one of the easiest, quickest, most economical and delicious appetizers you can serve. If you do have any leftover mushroom mixture (I doubt you will!) you can use it as a sauce over almost anything else.

❖❖❖

4	**cups cooked couscous or rice**
3	**large onions, sliced**
1	**large can or $^1/_2$ pound fresh, sliced mushrooms**
	Salt and pepper to taste
2–3	**tablespoons margarine**

❖❖❖

1. Saute onions in margarine until limp and almost golden.
2. Add mushrooms and saute for a minute or two; then cover and simmer for about 5 minutes.
3. Serve over cooked couscous or rice.

Sweet and Sour Meatballs

Meat
6 servings

This recipe can be used as an appetizer or a main course. If you are going to serve it as an appetizer, make the meatballs smaller and serve over rice.

❖❖❖

2	**pounds ground beef**
1	**tablespoon seasoned bread crumbs**
1	**egg**
	Salt and pepper to taste
1	**(12 ounce) bottle chili sauce**
	Juice of ¹/₂ lemon
1	**(10 ounce) jar grape or apricot jelly**

❖❖❖

1. Combine meat, bread crumbs, egg and salt and pepper in a mixing bowl.
2. Moisten hands with cold water, then form mixture into small balls and set aside.
3. Place chili sauce, lemon juice, salt and jelly in a large saucepan and bring to a boil.
4. Carefully add meatballs and allow to simmer 45 minutes, covered.

❖ This recipe can be made the day before and refrigerated. The hardened fat can then be removed and discarded.

❖ Freezes well.

❖ To stretch, add ¹/₂ to ³/₄ cup raw rice to meatball mixture before shaping into balls.

Chapter Seven
BREAD

There are very few foods as tempting as freshly baked bread. Homemade bread is not only delicious, it also does wonders for the budget.

Bread is basically a mixture of flour, yeast, liquid, sugar, salt and oil. Other ingredients are what make for variations on the theme.

If you've never made bread before, don't be intimidated. Even children love to make bread and quickly become very good at it. It's easy, it's fun and nothing feels better than having family and guests compliment you on your homemade bread.

When baking bread, it is necessary to remove a small amount of the dough (called *separating challah*) and say the appropriate blessing.

Some tips for success:

1. Yeast is a living organism. Don't use fresh yeast after its expiration date. Always test (proof) the yeast first. It's very frustrating to wait for an hour or so for your bread to rise only to find it isn't rising because the yeast wasn't good.

2. To dissolve and proof yeast, pour 105°–115° water into a small bowl. Test it on your wrist: it should feel pleasantly warm, not hot. If the water is any hotter, it will kill the yeast. (The amount of water will be specified in each recipe.) Add the yeast, a pinch of sugar, and a pinch of flour. Allow to stand 5 – 10 minutes. If the mixture doesn't become foamy, throw it out and start over with fresh yeast.

3. For a change of pace, try substituting water in which potatoes have been cooked for the liquid in your recipe (the potato starch adds flavor and elasticity to kneaded dough). Just about any liquid can be substituted for any other liquid in breadmaking.

4. When a recipe gives a range in the amount of flour to be added during beating, start with the smaller amount. Add only enough extra flour to keep the dough from being sticky and to keep it manageable. Excess flour gives bread a heavy texture.

5. The best temperature for raising dough is 80°– 85°. If you have a gas oven with a pilot light, this is an ideal place for dough raising. Don't put the dough in a hot oven to rise because excessive heat will kill the yeast.

6. If the dough doesn't seem to rise, place it in the microwave on defrost cycle for about two minutes. Let it rest, then "defrost" again for another two minutes, then let it sit. If, after about half an hour the dough still hasn't risen, throw it away and start again. If you're sure the yeast was fresh, you may have killed it with water that was too hot.

7. To help the dough rise evenly, make sure the ends of the dough touch the ends of the pan. Fill the pans $^1/_3$ to $^2/_3$ full. Braided bread should be braided very loosely so that the interwoven effect is not lost as the baking bread expands.

8. Recipes will generally say, "let rise...until doubled". The time it takes to double can vary greatly depending on the weather and the humidity. But be sure to let it rise until it really has doubled in size.

9. If you are using a glass pan, reduce the oven temperature by 25°. As soon as the bread is done, remove the loaves from the pan and place on wire racks to cool. This prevents the bottom and side crusts from steaming and becoming soggy.

10. To obtain a soft, shiny crust, brush the loaves with margarine after baking. To obtain a glossy, crisp crust, brush loaves *before* baking with an egg beaten with one tablespoon of water.

11. Bread freezes beautifully. However, once it is thawed, it deteriorates faster than if it had not been frozen at all. For best results, wrap bread in air-tight foil before freezing and then put it in a plastic bag with all the air squeezed out. Be sure the bag is sealed tightly.

Amy's Challah

❖ **Notes** ❖

A hearty and flavorful challah. I like to make it using half stone-ground whole wheat flour and half white flour. The stone-ground flour gives it a wonderful taste but if used for more than half the necessary flour, the challah will be too heavy.

❖❖❖

4 cups whole wheat flour, preferably stone ground	1 1/2 cups warm water
4 cups white flour	1/3 cup oil
1 cup sugar	
1 1/2 tablespoons salt	**Topping:**
1 package dry yeast	1 egg, beaten
1/2 cup warm water	1 teaspoon sugar
3 eggs, beaten	1/4 teaspoon salt
	2 teaspoons water

❖❖❖

1. Mix flours, sugar and salt in large bowl or the bowl of your mixer.
2. Make a well in flour mixture and add yeast and 1/2 cup warm water. Leave for 15 minutes, or until yeast begins to bubble.
3. Add eggs, additional warm water and oil and knead for 15 minutes by hand or 7 – 8 minutes in the mixer.
4. Let rise 1 1/2 hours.
5. Punch down and knead briefly again.
6. Braid and let rise 1/2 hour.
7. Mix topping ingredients and pour or brush over loaves when ready to bake.
8. Bake in a 325° oven for 1/2 hour.
9. Challah is done when it is golden brown and sounds hollow when tapped on the bottom.
10. Cool on wire rack.

No-Knead Challah

Perfect for busy (or lazy) people because there's no need to knead this dough. You can start it, keep the dough in the refrigerator and bake it at your convenience.

❖❖❖

12	cups whole wheat flour
1¹/₂	packages dry, instant yeast
2	tablespoons salt
6	eggs
1	cup honey
1¹/₃	cups oil
2³/₄	cups hot water

❖❖❖

1. Mix together flour, yeast and salt in a large bowl.
2. Mix together eggs, honey, oil and hot water. Combine with dry ingredients.
3. Place dough in greased bowl and let rise until doubled in size, several hours or overnight in refrigerator.
4. Punch down, divide dough and braid.
5. Let rise again for ¹/₂ hour. Brush with beaten egg mixed with 1 tablespoon water.
6. Bake in a 350° oven for 30 minutes.
7. Challah is done when it is golden brown and sounds hollow when tapped on the bottom.
8. Cool on wire rack.

Aunt Esther's Challah

❖ **Notes** ❖

A tender, light and crusty challah. If using a mixer, knead half the dough at a time.

❖❖❖

3 **packages dry yeast**	**¹/₈ teaspoon saffron dissolved in**
2¹/₂ **cups warm water**	**1 tablespoon warm water**
¹/₂ **cup sugar**	1 **cup oil**
14 **cups sifted flour (3¹/₂ pounds)**	6 **eggs**
2 **tablespoons salt**	**Poppy or sesame seeds, optional**

❖❖❖

1. Dissolve yeast in 1 cup warm water with a pinch of sugar. Let sit about 10 minutes until it bubbles.
2. Meanwhile, sift flour, salt and remaining sugar together in a very large bowl.
3. Add the bubbly yeast, saffron, oil, 5 eggs and the remaining water into the flour mixture.
4. Knead on a floured surface until smooth and elastic. The dough should not stick to the hands or board. If it does, sprinkle small amounts of flour on dough until it no longer sticks.
5. Return dough to the bowl and brush the top with oil. Turn it over in the bowl and brush the top with oil again.
6. Cover with a damp towel and set in a warm place to rise for 1 hour or a little longer, until dough has doubled in size.
7. Punch down and let rise again for about 30 minutes.

(recipe continued...)

Aunt Esther's Challah... *(recipe continued...)*

8. Divide dough into four equal parts to make four loaves of challah. Smaller challahs or rolls can be made according to the family's needs or tastes.
9. Braid challahs and place on greased cookie sheets. Let rise again for half an hour.
10. Beat remaining egg and mix with 2 tablespoons water. "Paint" challahs with beaten egg and sprinkle with seeds, if desired.
11. Bake on lower shelf of a 350° oven for 30 minutes. If the top browns too quickly, cover with half of a large brown paper bag.
12. Challah is done when it is golden brown and sounds hollow when tapped on the bottom.
13. Cool on wire rack.

Cinnamon-Raisin Challah

Parve
1 large challah

❖ **Notes** ❖

This challah is wonderful with dairy meals. I like to serve it on Shavuot.

❖❖❖

4¹/₂	cups flour	1	cup hot tap water
2	tablespoons sugar	3	eggs, room temperature,
2	tablespoons honey		plus 1 egg white
1	tablespoon salt	1	teaspoon vanilla
1	package dry yeast	1	cup raisins
¹/₂	teaspoon cinnamon	1	egg yolk
¹/₄	teaspoon baking powder	2	tablespoons cold water
¹/₃	cup parve margarine, softened		

❖❖❖

1. In a large mixer bowl thoroughly mix 1¹/₄ cups flour with the sugar, honey, salt, yeast, cinnamon and baking powder.
2. Add softened margarine.
3. Gradually add very hot tap water to dry ingredients and beat two minutes at medium speed, scraping bowl occasionally.
4. Add 3 eggs and 1 egg white, vanilla and ¹/₂ cup flour, or enough to make a thick batter.
5. Beat at high speed for 2 minutes, scraping bowl occasionally.
6. Turn mixture out onto lightly floured board; knead until smooth and elastic (8–10 minutes).
7. Knead in raisins.
8. Place dough in greased bowl and turn to grease top.
9. Cover and let rise until doubled in bulk, about 1 hour.
10. Punch down and turn out onto lightly floured board.

❖ Start with 4¹/₂ cups flour and if dough is too sticky add up to an additional ¹/₂ cup.

(Recipe continued...)

Cinnamon-Raisin Challah... *(Recipe continued...)*

11. Divide dough in half and braid.
12. Place on large greased sheet, cover and let rise again (about 1 hour).
13. Beat egg yolk and cold water together and brush on loaves.
14. Bake in a 375° oven for about 30 minutes. Challah is done when it is golden brown and sounds hollow when tapped on the bottom.
15. Cool on wire rack.

Bubble Bread

Parve
60 rolls

❖❖❖

1	cup mashed potatoes	1	package yeast
1	cup water in which potatoes were cooked	$^1/_2$	cup lukewarm water
		2	eggs, well beaten
$^2/_3$	cup margarine or shortening	5–6	cups flour
$^2/_3$	cup sugar	$^1/_2$	cup melted parve margarine
1	teaspoon salt		

❖❖❖

1. Combine hot potato water, potatoes, margarine, sugar and salt in a large mixing bowl. Let stand until lukewarm.
2. Add yeast to $^1/_2$ cup lukewarm water and let it dissolve.
3. Add eggs and about $1^1/_2$ cups flour to potato mixture and beat well.
4. Add additional flour to make a stiff dough.
5. Turn out onto board and knead thoroughly, or knead in mixer.
6. Return to a greased bowl and turn dough to grease top. Cover with a damp cloth and let rise until doubled in size.
7. Punch down, cover, and put into refrigerator to chill for several hours.
8. Remove from refrigerator and roll dough to about $^1/_2$ inch thickness. Cut into biscuit-sized rounds.
9. Dip rounds in hot melted margarine and place 4 – 5 across in a 9×13-inch pan. Let rise until doubled in size, covered with a towel in a draft-free place.
10. Bake in a 325° oven for 15 – 20 minutes.
11. Invert on a rack to cool. Break apart to freeze.

❖ These rolls freeze very well.

Bagels

Although bagels are readily available, they can be quite expensive to buy. They are very easy to make, and 4¹/₂ cups of flour will make approximately two dozen bagels. (Your kids will love making them and you can stock your freezer with them.)

❖❖❖

1 **cup warm water**	3 **teaspoons sugar**
4¹/₂ **cups flour**	2 **tablespoons oil**
1 **package dry yeast**	2 **eggs**
2 **teaspoons salt**	

❖❖❖

1. Place water, 1 cup of the flour, sugar and yeast in a large bowl. Mix well and let sit for about 15 minutes until it begins to bubble.
2. Add the remaining flour and other ingredients and knead until smooth and elastic.
3. Place dough in lightly oiled bowl or plastic bag, turning to cover all the dough with oil. Refrigerate dough overnight.
4. The next day, remove dough from refrigerator and divide into 24 pieces. Roll each piece into a rope about 6 inches long. Wind the rope into a circle and press to join the ends together.
5. Place on floured surface and repeat with remaining pieces of dough. Cover with a damp towel and let rise until bagels have risen somewhat but are not puffy (about one hour).
6. Bring a large pot of water to a boil and boil the bagels, a few at a time, for 2 minutes, turning them over with a slotted spoon as they rise to the top.
7. Remove from water and drain. Repeat with remaining bagels. At this point, you can dip the tops of the bagels into poppy seeds, sesame seeds or salt if you wish.
8. Place boiled bagels on a floured baking sheet and bake for one minute in a pre-heated 500° oven.
9. Turn and bake on the other side for 15 minutes until a rich shiny brown.

Homemade Biscuit Mix

Dairy or Parve
15 cups

This mixture is very economical to make, and can be prepared ahead of time and used as a base for many casseroles, desserts and other dishes. See the variations following this recipe.

❖❖❖

12	cups flour
¹/₄	cup baking powder
2	tablespoons salt
1	pound vegetable shortening

❖❖❖

❖ If lighter, fluffier biscuits are desired, substitute milk for the water, decrease baking temperature by 50°, and increase baking time by approximately 4 minutes.

❖ If drop biscuits are desired, increase the water slightly to produce a softer dough. Drop onto a greased baking sheet.

❖ You can use this mix in the following recipes listed in this book:
  · Almond Pudding Cake
  · Biscuits
  · Muffins
  · Easy Lasagna Squares
  · French Apple Pie
  · Impossibly Easy Pizza

1. Mix together the flour, baking powder and salt in a large bowl.
2. Add vegetable shortening and blend together with a pastry blender, two knives, or your fingertips, until mixture is the same texture as coarse cornmeal.
3. Store in a dry cool place.

To make biscuits:

1. Combine 1 cup mix and ¹/₄ cup liquid (water or milk). Stir with fork just until dry ingredients are moistened and dough forms a ball.
2. Knead dough on lightly floured surface 8 – 10 times.
3. Roll out with a rolling pin and cut with a floured glass or cookie cutter.
4. Place on an ungreased baking sheet and bake in a preheated 400° oven for 10 – 12 minutes or until lightly browned.
5. Cool slightly on wire rack.

To make muffins:

1. Combine 2¼ cups of biscuit mix with ¼ cup of sugar, 1 egg, ¾ cup water and 1 tablespoon oil. Stir just until moistened. Batter should be lumpy.
2. Add nuts, cinnamon, raisins, blueberries or other fruit if desired.
3. Fill greased muffin pans ⅔ full and bake at 350° for 15 minutes or bake in a 9×12-inch greased baking pan.

To make dumplings:

1. Combine 2 cups of mix with ⅔ cup of water and drop by tablespoons in a pot full of lightly simmering stew.
2. Cook rapidly, uncovered for 10 minutes, then cover and cook for an additional 10 – 12 minutes.

❖ Notes ❖

Apple Spice Muffins

❖❖❖

³/₄ **cup apple juice**
1   **egg, beaten**
¹/₄ **cup melted parve margarine**

2   **cups flour**
¹/₂ **cup sugar**
1   **tablespoon baking powder**
¹/₂ **teaspoon salt**
1   **teaspoon cinnamon**
1   **cup finely chopped apples**
¹/₄ **cup raisins**

❖❖❖

1. Preheat oven to 400°.
2. Add juice to egg and stir in margarine.
3. Mix dry ingredients thoroughly; stir in chopped apples and raisins.
4. Add liquid mixture and stir just until most of the dry ingredients are moistened. Do not overmix. Batter should be lumpy.
5. Fill greased muffin tins ²/₃ full.
6. Bake 20 – 25 minutes or until golden brown.

Banana Bran Muffins

Dairy
12 muffins

❖❖❖

1   cup All-Bran cereal
1   cup milk (or juice)
3   tablespoons oil
1   egg
1$^1/_4$ cups flour
2   tablespoons flour
2   tablespoons sugar
1   tablespoon baking powder
$^1/_4$ teaspoon salt
$^3/_4$ cup mashed ripe bananas
$^1/_2$ cup raisins
     Maple syrup

❖❖❖

1. Preheat oven to 400°.
2. Grease 12-cup muffin tin, or line with muffin papers.
3. Stir cereal into milk in a large bowl and let stand two minutes.
4. Beat in oil and egg.
5. Combine flour, sugar, baking powder and salt in another bowl. Stir into cereal mixture.
6. Add banana and raisins and mix just to combine.
7. Spoon batter into prepared tin. Lightly drizzle tops with maple syrup.
8. Bake until lightly browned, about 30 minutes. Best served immediately.

Oatmeal Muffins

Parve
12 muffins

❖❖❖

1	cup uncooked oatmeal
1	cup orange juice
$^1/_2$	cup firmly packed brown sugar
$^1/_2$	cup oil
1	egg, beaten
1	cup flour
1	teaspoon baking powder
$^1/_2$	teaspoon baking soda
$^1/_2$	teaspoon salt

❖❖❖

1. Combine oatmeal and orange juice and let sit for 30 minutes.
2. Preheat oven to 400°. Generously grease a 12-muffin tin.
3. Blend sugar, oil and egg into oatmeal mixture.
4. Add remaining ingredients and stir until just moistened.
5. Spoon into prepared tin, filling cups $^2/_3$ full.
6. Bake until muffins are golden brown and toothpick inserted in centers comes out clean, about 20 minutes. Cool 5 minutes and remove from tin.

Seasoned Bread Crumbs

Parve
2 ¹/₂ *cups*

Quick, easy to make, and great to have on hand to bread chicken or fish, or to use in any recipe calling for bread crumbs.

❖❖❖

4   slices stale bread, cubed
¹/₃   cup instant minced onion
1   tablespoon dried parsley
1   tablespoon garlic salt or
         seasoned salt
¹/₂   teaspoon pepper
1   teaspoon oregano

❖❖❖

1. Combine all ingredients in bowl of food processor and process until bread crumbs are fine.
2. Store in an airtight container.

❖ Use within six months.

Carrot Bread

Parve
1 loaf

You can also substitute zucchini for the carrots with wonderful results.

❖❖❖

$^1/_2$	cup parve margarine, softened
$^1/_2$	cup sugar
$^1/_2$	cup brown sugar
3	eggs
2	cups flour
1	teaspoon baking powder
1	teaspoon baking soda
1	teaspoon salt
2	teaspoons cinnamon
3	cups grated carrots
1	cup coarsely chopped walnuts or pecans

❖❖❖

1. Lightly grease a large loaf pan.
2. In mixer, cream margarine with sugars and beat until fluffy.
3. Add eggs and beat well.
4. Mix dry ingredients and add to egg and sugar mixture.
5. Fold in carrots and nuts. Mix thoroughly.
6. Pour into prepared pan and bake for 1 hour at 350°. Remove from oven and cool on rack.

Chapter Eight
Soup

Soup is one of the greatest things to happen to a budget. It's delicious, nutritious, filling, easy to make and inexpensive.

Soup is also one of the most comforting of foods. On a cold winter evening, there's nothing better than a thick, hot soup, bread and a salad. And, in the hot days of summer, a chilled soup is delightfully refreshing.

One of the simplest, most inexpensive and fun ideas for serving a large group of people is to set out a buffet of different soups, along with a huge tossed salad and a basket of breads and muffins. This meal can even be served from the stove for a casual dinner. Let your guests come into the kitchen and serve themselves. They'll love being able to sample all the soups.

On your busy days, don't forget about the electric crock pot. Simply place all the soup ingredients into the pot, set it and you have dinner ready when you return home.

Suggestions:

Here's a lovely way to "dress-up" and serve soup:

1. Place soup in an oven-proof mug or bowl.
2. Roll out puff pastry and cut into circles 2 inches wider than the top of the soup mugs.
3. Place each circle of uncooked pastry over the top of the mug, sealing it along the sides with water or egg white.
4. Preheat oven to 425° and place mugs on a cookie sheet.

5. Bake for about 15 minutes until crust is puffed and golden. It is best served immediately but can remain in a slightly warm oven.

You can also fill the mugs with soup, top with pastry and refrigerate until you're ready to bake and serve. Be careful of the hot mug!

In all the following soup recipes, parve bouillon (beef or chicken flavored) can be substituted for actual beef or chicken broth. You can also substitute parve cream for dairy cream or sour cream. Another option, to give the soup a creamy consistency, is to simply puree some of the vegetables from the soup and add the puree back into the pot.

Sometimes soups don't turn out the way you want. If your soup is too . . .

Thick: Warm it up before you do anything else. The soup may have just solidified when refrigerated. If the soup is still too thick, simply add water or broth, a little at a time, until reaching the consistency you want.

Thin: Just add instant mashed potatoes (I always keep a package on hand), a tablespoon or two at a time, until the soup reaches the desired consistency.

Or, mix a tablespoon or two of cornstarch or flour into a little cold soup or water, and add this to soup. Add a little more if you see that it hasn't thickened enough.

For a quick and easy thickener, puree some of the vegetables in a food processor and return to the soup.

Salty: Adding raw, peeled potatoes can save an over-salted soup! You'll only need one or two — potatoes can absorb a lot of salt. Simmer the soup until the potatoes are tender.

Fatty: Chill the soup in the refrigerator until fat congeals on the top of the pot and then remove it with a spoon. If you are short on time, lay a paper towel on the surface and, as it absorbs the fat, replace it with a fresh one.

Curried Carrot Soup

Parve or Meat
4 servings

Guests love it when I serve this soup at Shabbat meals during the summer.

❖❖❖

1	medium onion, coarsely chopped
2	tablespoons parve margarine
4	carrots, coarsely chopped
4	cups chicken broth or bouillon (parve or meat)
1	1×2-inch strip lemon rind
2	teaspoons sugar
$^3/_4$	teaspoon curry powder

$^1/_4$	teaspoon salt
$^1/_4$	teaspoon pepper
3	tablespoons dry white wine

Optional garnish:
Toasted chopped almonds,
3 finely chopped green onions
Thin sliced carrot strips

❖❖❖

1. Saute onion in margarine in a large skillet until tender.
2. Add remaining ingredients except garnishes.
3. Reduce heat. Cover and simmer 20 minutes or until carrots are tender. Let cool.
4. Pour half of mixture into blender or food processor and process until smooth. Pour into bowl or pitcher, and repeat with remaining mixture.
5. Stir in wine.
6. Cover and chill.
7. Garnish, if desired, and serve cold.

❖ **Notes** ❖

Black Bean Soup

Meat
12 servings

Although this soup simmers for a long time, it doesn't have to be watched. I like to make it on a day when I'm home doing chores.

❖❖❖

4	cups black beans	2	teaspoons salt
4	quarts water	$^1/_4$	teaspoon pepper, or to taste
2	tablespoons parve margarine	1	tablespoon parve margarine
1	small onion, diced	2	tablespoons flour
2	ribs celery, diced		Garnish: 1 onion, finely chopped
4	hot dogs		

❖❖❖

1. Rinse beans, place in a large bowl, and cover with water. Set aside and allow to soak overnight.
2. Next day, drain and place the black beans in a soup pot. Add water and simmer, covered, for 2 hours, or until beans are almost tender.
3. Melt margarine in a skillet, add onion and celery and saute until limp. Add to beans.
4. Add hot dogs.
5. Simmer 1 hour, covered, then remove and refrigerate hot dogs.
6. Cover soup and continue cooking until beans are soft (approximately 4 hours).
7. Add salt and pepper.
8. Melt margarine in small saucepan, add flour and stir until blended.
9. Cook over low heat, stirring constantly. Slowly add one cup of hot soup, blending well.
10. Pour this mixture back into the soup pot.
11. Thinly slice the hot dogs, add to soup and simmer about 10 minutes, or until thick.
12. Garnish bowl of soup with 1 tablespoon chopped onion.

Quick 'n' Easy Bean Soup

Parve
4 servings

I first tasted this soup at my gourmet dinner club. When I got the recipe from my friend, I couldn't believe how simple it was to make.

❖❖❖

1	medium onion
3	tablespoons oil
2	cups parve beef bouillon
1	12-ounce can vegetarian beans
1	small can tomato paste
3	garlic cloves, minced
	A dash of pepper
1	teaspoon salt
$^1/_4$	cup fresh parsley, minced
	Oregano to taste

❖❖❖

1. Chop onion coarsely and saute in oil until golden.
2. Add remaining ingredients and 4 cups of water.
3. Bring to a boil, lower heat, and simmer 20 minutes.

Golden Chicken Soup I

This recipe uses various chicken parts and lots of vegetables. I serve the chicken necks and gizzards to those who like them.

❖❖❖

3	**pounds any combination of chicken necks, backs and/or gizzards**
4–6	**quarts water**
4	**medium whole onions, peeled**
4–6	**large thick carrots, peeled**
4	**ribs celery, cut into large pieces**
1–2	**cloves garlic, chopped**
4	**large whole zucchini**

A large handful of fresh dill, chopped (preferably) or
2 **tablespoons dried**
A large handful of fresh parsley, cut in half, or
2 **tablespoons dried**
2 **teaspoons salt, or to taste**
1 **teaspoon white pepper, or to taste**
2 **tablespoons chicken bouillon***

*If necessary to strengthen soup

❖❖❖

1. Rinse chicken necks and gizzards and trim off excess fat. Remove skin from backs.
2. Place in a large soup pot and cover with water.
3. Bring to a boil and skim surface.
4. Add onions, carrots, celery and garlic. Cover and simmer for approximately 2 hours.
5. Add zucchini, dill, parsley, and salt and pepper. Continue simmering, covered, until zucchini is tender, about 20 – 30 minutes.
6. Taste to adjust seasonings if necessary.
7. Remove chicken from soup.
8. If you prefer a clear broth, gently remove vegetables from soup and strain soup. Return strained liquid to pot and replace vegetables. Add necks and gizzards.
9. Allow soup to cool and then refrigerate.
10. When fat is congealed, skim from the top of soup and discard.
11. Reheat soup before serving.

❖ Notes ❖

❖ Whenever you buy a chicken, save the neck and put it in a separate bag in the freezer. When the bag gets filled, use it to make soup.

❖ Necks and backs are incredibly inexpensive to buy. In fact, some butchers will give you the backs for free.

❖ Place the chicken pieces in a net bag before placing in the soup. When the soup is cooked, simply lift the bag out of the pot.

Golden Chicken Soup II

Meat
10 servings

This recipe makes a clear soup, using a whole plump chicken. I set the cooked chicken aside to make a main course dish.

❖❖❖

1	4–5 pound chicken	3–4	zucchini, sliced
4	quarts water	4–5	stalks fresh dill weed
2	large onions, peeled	1	tablespoon salt
4	ribs celery	$^1/_2$	teaspoon white pepper
4–6	carrots, peeled	1–2	tablespoons chicken bouillon
1–2	cloves garlic, chopped		*If necessary to strengthen soup

❖❖❖

1. Rinse chicken and trim off excess fat. Check skin for pinfeathers and remove.
2. Place chicken, onions, celery, carrots and garlic in a large soup pot and cover with water.
3. Bring to a boil and simmer several hours, until chicken is tender.
4. Skim the scum from surface of soup.
5. Add zucchini, dill weed, salt and pepper and simmer until zucchini is tender, about half an hour.
6. Taste to adjust seasonings.
7. Remove chicken and vegetables from soup, strain soup. Discard onions and celery. Return carrots and zucchini to soup.
8. Allow to cool and refrigerate.
9. When fat is congealed, remove from top of soup and discard (or, reserve fat to be used as schmaltz).
10. Reheat before serving.

Cream of Cauliflower Soup

Dairy or Parve
6 servings

❖❖❖

2	tablespoons margarine
1/2	small onion, thinly sliced
4	cups parve bouillon
1	pound bag frozen cauliflower, coarsely chopped
1	large potato, peeled and coarsely chopped
1	bay leaf
1	cup half-and-half or parve cream
2	tablespoons grated carrot
1	teaspoon salt or to taste
1/4	teaspoon fresh ground pepper, or to taste

Garnish: minced fresh parsley

❖❖❖

1. Melt margarine in a large, heavy saucepan.
2. Add onion and saute until soft and translucent, about 5 minutes. Do not brown.
3. Add bouillon, cauliflower, potato and bay leaf and bring to a boil.
4. Reduce heat, cover and simmer until vegetables are soft, about 15 minutes.
5. Remove and discard bay leaf and cool soup.
6. Puree soup in batches in blender until smooth.
7. Return to saucepan. Stir in half-and-half or parve cream, add carrot and heat.
8. Season with salt and pepper.
9. Garnish with parsley.

Cream of Cucumber Soup

Dairy or Parve
6 servings

A delightfully refreshing cold summer soup.

❖❖❖

3	medium cucumbers
3	tablespoons margarine
$^1/_2$	cup onion, chopped
4	cups chicken-flavored bouillon
1	teaspoon garlic salt
4	tablespoons lemon juice
$^1/_2$	teaspoon dill weed
$1^1/_2$	cups sour cream or parve cream

❖❖❖

1. Peel two of the three cucumbers and cut in half lengthwise. Scoop out seeds, and thinly slice.
2. Melt margarine in pot.
3. Add onion, cucumber slices and saute until soft.
4. Add chicken-flavored bouillon, cover and simmer for 10 minutes.
5. Remove from heat, add garlic salt, lemon juice, and dill.
6. Allow the soup to cool slightly, then add the sour cream or parve cream.
7. Place small amounts of mixture in a blender or food processor and puree.
8. Cut remaining cucumber in half, peel one half and seed. Coarsely chop and add to soup.
9. Chill thoroughly.
10. Take remaining cucumber, score with prongs of a fork and thinly slice.
11. To serve, float slices of cucumber in each bowl and sprinkle with additional dill.

Fresh Mushroom Soup

Parve
6 servings

A very elegant soup.

❖❖❖

¹/₄	**cup parve margarine**
¹/₄	**pound fresh mushrooms, thinly sliced**
¹/₃	**cup finely chopped onion**
1	**clove garlic, minced**
1	**tablespoon fresh lemon juice**
3	**tablespoons flour**
4	**cups parve chicken-flavored bouillon**
2	**teaspoons salt**
¹/₄	**teaspoon ground pepper**
2	**cups parve cream**
	Garnish:
	chopped parsley

❖❖❖

1. Heat margarine in large saucepan.
2. Saute mushrooms, onion and garlic 4 – 5 minutes, stirring constantly.
3. Sprinkle with the lemon juice.
4. Blend in flour.
5. Gradually stir in bouillon, salt and pepper.
6. Cook over medium heat, stirring constantly until mixture is slightly thickened.
7. Stir in cream and heat. *Do not boil.*
8. Garnish with chopped parsley.

Onion Soup

Dairy or Parve
6 servings

❖❖❖

12 onions, thinly sliced
4   tablespoons margarine
4   cups parve beef-flavored
       bouillon
1   teaspoon Worcestershire sauce
¹/₄ teaspoon hot pepper sauce
6   1-inch slices French bread
6   tablespoons grated parmesan
       cheese (if making dairy)
    A dash of ground black pepper

❖❖❖

1. Saute onions in margarine in a large saucepan for 15 minutes, or until golden brown.
2. Add bouillon, Worcestershire sauce, and hot pepper.
3. Bring to a boil, reduce heat, cover and simmer for 4 hours.
4. Toast French bread in toaster oven until brown on both sides.
5. Sprinkle each slice with 1 tablespoon grated cheese.
6. Broil under low heat until cheese is browned.
7. Serve toast with soup.

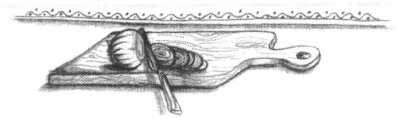

❖ If serving soup with a meat meal, omit French bread and cheese and put soup in oven-proof bowl or mug. Place square of defrosted puff pastry over bowl and seal edges. Place bowl in preheated 425° oven until pastry is puffed and golden.

Stone Soup

There is a traditional children's story about a beggar who asks a woman for some food. When she refuses, he offers to teach her to make a pot of soup from just a pot of water and a stone...and then asks her for a pinch of this and a handful of that. The woman is amazed that he can turn out such a wonderful soup from just a stone and water!

This soup starts out with just a turkey carcass...and a pinch of this and a handful of that.

❖❖❖

Carcass of one cooked turkey
3   **cups cold chicken broth**
3   **cups cold beef broth**
4   **cups cold water**
1   **pound onions, chopped**
5–6 **carrots, peeled**
5–6 **stalks celery, sliced**
2   **teaspoons salt, or to taste**
$^1/_2$ **teaspoon fresh black pepper**
$1^1/_2$ **cups barley, rinsed**
1   **stone (optional)**

❖❖❖

1. In an 8-quart pot, place bones, broths and water.
2. Bring to a boil, skimming off the froth as it rises to the top of the pot.
3. Add the rest of the ingredients, except the barley.
4. Cover and simmer for 2 hours.
5. Add barley, taste and correct the seasonings.
6. Simmer an additional hour, covered.
7. Remove and discard bones. Cool and skim the fat from the top.
8. Reheat and serve.

❖ Save your turkey carcasses in the freezer for this soup.

Split Pea Soup

❖❖❖

1   onion, diced
2   tablespoons oil
1   bay leaf
1   teaspoon celery seed
1½ cups split peas
½   cup barley
½   cup lima beans
3   quarts water
2   teaspoons salt
    A dash of pepper
1   teaspoon basil
1   teaspoon thyme
2–3 carrots, sliced
3   stalks celery, sliced
½   cup fresh parsley, chopped
1   potato, diced

❖❖❖

1. Saute onion in oil until soft.
2. Add bay leaf, celery seed, split peas, barley and lima beans.
3. Add water and bring to a boil. Lower heat, cover and simmer approximately 1½ hours.
4. Add remaining ingredients and cook another 30 – 45 minutes.

❖ **Notes** ❖

❖ If you are pressed for time, this soup can be made in an electric crockpot. Simply combine the ingredients and cook all day.

Cold Strawberry Soup

Dairy or Parve
6 servings

You'll want to serve this again and again when lush, ripe strawberries are in season. It looks lovely and the taste is exceptional.

❖❖❖

1	cup sugar
1	cup water
$^1/_2$	cup cornstarch
1	tablespoon vanilla
$1^1/_2$	cups grape juice or wine
2	pint containers strawberries
$^1/_4$	cup lemon juice
$^1/_2$	cup orange juice concentrate
$1^1/_2$	cups additional juice (grape, orange or apple)
2	cups sour cream or yogurt (optional)

❖❖❖

1. Mix sugar and cornstarch, then add additional juice and water.
2. Bring to a boil, stirring constantly, until thickened.
3. Remove from heat and add vanilla.
4. Set aside about $^1/_2$ container of the prettiest strawberries for garnish and mash the remainder.
5. Add lemon juice and orange juice concentrate to mashed strawberries.
6. Add to soup mixture.
7. Add remaining juice or wine until desired consistency is reached.
8. Sour cream or yogurt can be added to the soup at this point if you like.
9. Chill and serve, topped with strawberry slices.

Ten-Layer Vegetable Soup

Parve
8 servings

❖ **Notes** ❖

This meal-in-itself soup is so satisfyingly quick and easy to make, it will become a family favorite. The vegetables can be changed to suit your taste or what you have available.

❖❖❖

2 tablespoons olive oil	1 large zucchini, cubed
2 tomatoes, cut into $^1/_4$-inch slices	$^1/_4$ teaspoon hot paprika
2 onions, cut into $^1/_4$-inch slices	2 cups frozen peas
$^1/_4$ teaspoon ground allspice	2 cups frozen lima beans
2 cloves garlic, minced	2 teaspoons mixed chopped fresh herbs (sage, chives, thyme, and/or rosemary)
1 head Romaine lettuce, shredded	
$^1/_2$ cup bulgur wheat	6 cups parve chicken-flavored bouillon
1 cup fresh parsley, chopped	
$^1/_2$ cup chopped fresh basil, or 2 tablespoons dried	1 tablespoon salt
	$^1/_2$ teaspoon pepper, or to taste

❖❖❖

1. Spread oil over bottom of a large soup pot and layer all ingredients in pot except for chicken bouillon and herbs.

2. Cover and cook over medium heat for 15 minutes.

3. Remove cover, add bouillon and herbs.

4. Bring to a boil, then reduce heat and simmer, uncovered, for $^1/_2$ hour.

5. Season with salt and pepper to taste.

Aunt Esther's Kreplach

❖ **Notes** ❖

Whenever I make kreplach I always double the recipe and freeze half.

❖❖❖

Filling:

1/2 pound cooked meat or chicken, chopped

1 medium onion, chopped

2 hard-boiled eggs

1 rib celery, chopped

1 raw egg

Approximately 3 tablespoons chicken fat or oil

1 teaspoon salt, or to taste

1/4 teaspoon pepper, or to taste

Dough:

1 egg

2 tablespoons water

1/4 teaspoon salt

1 1/2 cups flour

❖❖❖

1. Place meat or chicken in bowl of food processor.
2. Add onion, hard-boiled eggs, celery and chop.
3. Transfer to another bowl and add raw egg and enough fat or oil to hold mixture together.
4. Add salt and pepper, to taste.
5. Cover and refrigerate.
6. In a medium-sized bowl beat egg and water together.
7. Mix salt with flour and gradually add to egg.
8. Knead until dough becomes smooth.
9. Lightly flour clean counter and roll dough to 1/8 inch thickness. Cut into 2-inch squares. Keep unused dough covered with a damp towel while assembling kreplach to keep it from drying out.

(Recipe continued...)

Aunt Esther's Kreplach... *(Recipe continued...)*

10. Place 1 teaspoon of meat filling on each square. Fold left top corner of square to bottom right corner to form a triangle. Using the tines of a fork, firmly press edges together.
11. Drop into boiling, salted water, or soup, and cook approximately 15 – 20 minutes. Kreplach should rise to the top when done.

Variations:

Baked Kreplach: (may be served as an hors d'oeuvre)

1. Boil kreplach for 5 minutes.
2. Remove with a slotted spoon and place on a greased cookie sheet.
3. Bake in a preheated 350° oven until crisp.

Fried Kreplach:

1. Boil kreplach for 5 minutes.
2. Remove with a slotted spoon and drain on absorbent paper.
3. Fry in $1/2$ cup oil until browned and crisp.

Ravioli:

1. Boil prepared kreplach for 5 minutes, remove with a slotted spoon and drain.
2. Place in a large casserole, cover with spaghetti sauce.
3. Bake in a preheated 350° oven.

❖ To freeze kreplach, place them on a lightly greased cookie sheet, or one covered with waxed paper and freeze. When they are frozen, remove the kreplach from the cookie sheet and put them into a plastic bag or container and return them to the freezer. This method prevents the kreplach from sticking together.

Lentil Soup

My daughter Amy's favorite. I almost always have a batch of it simmering in my crock pot during the winter.

❖❖❖

1	package lentils (12–16 oz.)
3–4	carrots, sliced thin
3–4	stalks celery, sliced thin
1–2	onions, chopped
1–2	cloves garlic, chopped
1	bay leaf
	Salt and pepper, to taste
	Water to cover
2–3	beef bouillon cubes (parve or meat)
	Hot dogs, tongue (optional)

❖❖❖

1. Combine all ingredients, except bullion cubes and meat, in a soup pot.
2. Gently boil ingredients until lentils burst (several hours).
3. Add 2–3 bouillon cubes.
4. Cut up hot dogs and/or tongue and add to the soup and continue simmering until the lentils are soft.

Chapter Nine
SALADS

The price of vegetables fluctuates according to both season and the weather. Produce may be very reasonably priced one week, but may — because of unseasonal rains or drought somewhere — skyrocket the next week. Salads, if you're not careful, can become a very expensive part of the meal.

Be aware of prices and make your salads from ingredients that are sensibly priced that week. However, when you get to the store and see the actual prices, be flexible enough to change your plans if necessary.

Salads can be served as a separate course. An elegant way to serve a salad is to prepare and serve it on individual plates.

Layered Salad

Parve
8 servings

Use a clear glass or lucite bowl for serving this salad. The alternating brightly-colored layers will take this out of the category of an ordinary mixed salad and bring exclamations of delight from your guests.

❖❖❖

¹/₂	head lettuce, cleaned and coarsely shredded
1	whole lemon, seeded and chopped
5–6	carrots, thinly sliced
4–5	cucumbers, unpeeled and thinly sliced
5–6	tomatoes, in medium slices
3–4	green bell peppers, seeded and thinly sliced
2	cups frozen peas, defrosted but uncooked
1	can corn, drained
3	scallions, finely chopped

❖❖❖

1. Mix shredded lettuce with chopped lemon and place in bottom of bowl.
2. Layer vegetables in order given so that colored layers are obvious through the clear sides of the bowl.
3. Make circle of defrosted peas around the rim of salad bowl.
4. Fill center with drained corn.
5. Garnish with chopped green onion.
6. Serve with vinaigrette salad dressing on the side.

❖ Other vegetables of your choice can be substituted. The main point is to have layers of contrasting colors.

Tomato-Basil Salad

❖ **Notes** ❖

An all-time favorite with both family and guests. Fabulous when lush, ripe tomatoes are in season.

❖❖❖

4	medium tomatoes
6	tablespoons chopped fresh parsley
1	clove garlic
6	tablespoons olive oil
2	tablespoons white vinegar
1	teaspoon salt
1	tablespoon or more fresh chopped basil
$^1/_8$	teaspoon fresh ground pepper, or to taste
3	scallions, very finely chopped

❖❖❖

1. Slice tomatoes and layer with parsley in a serving bowl.
2. Mix remaining ingredients in blender or food processor and pour over tomatoes and parsley.
3. Serve garnished with chopped green onions.

Bean Sprout Salad

❖ **Notes** ❖

From a cooking class I called "Chinese on Ice". A cool, summer dish.

❖❖❖

$^1/_2$ **pound fresh bean sprouts**
1   **tablespoon oriental sesame oil**
$^1/_4$ **cup chopped scallions**
1   **tablespoon oil**
2   **tablespoons soy sauce**
1   **tablespoon red wine vinegar**
1   **teaspoon sugar**

❖❖❖

1. Soak bean sprouts in cold water and discard what floats to the top.
2. Drain bean spouts, place in salad bowl and top with scallions.
3. Combine remaining ingredients in a screw top jar and shake until smooth.
4. Pour over the salad, toss and serve.

Spicy Cucumber Salad

Parve
4 servings

Another refreshing "Chinese on Ice" creation.

❖❖❖

2	**medium cucumbers**
2	**teaspoons Oriental sesame seed oil**
1	**teaspoon soy sauce**
$^1/_4$	**teaspoon hot pepper sauce**
1	**tablespoon white vinegar**
$^1/_2$	**teaspoon salt**
1	**tablespoon sugar**

❖❖❖

1. Peel the cucumbers and cut them lengthwise in two.
2. With a small spoon, scrape the seeds out of each half, leaving hollow boat-like shells.
3. Cut the cucumbers crosswise into thin slices.
4. In a small bowl combine the remaining ingredients and mix well.
5. Add the cucumber and toss to coat each slice thoroughly with the dressing.
6. Chill slightly before serving.

Mediterranean Salad

❖ **Notes** ❖

I call this Mediterranean Salad because it was taught to me many years ago by an Israeli friend.

❖❖❖

$^1/_2$ head lettuce, chopped
2   cucumbers, chopped
1   large bell pepper, chopped
3   whole scallions, chopped
$^1/_3$ cup pitted green olives, sliced
$^1/_2$ cup pitted black olives, sliced
$^1/_3$ teaspoon garlic powder
1   teaspoon salt
1   teaspoon dried dill
  Dash each of:
    oregano
    parsley
    basil
    celery salt
    black pepper
$^1/_4$ cup olive oil
$^1/_4$ cup lemon juice

❖❖❖

❖ If you are making this salad ahead of time, add the olives, seasonings and dressing just before serving or it will get soggy.

1. Place vegetables and olives in a salad bowl.
2. Add seasonings, oil and lemon juice.
3. Toss, taste and adjust seasoning.

Middle-Eastern Rice Salad

Parve
6 servings

For variety, corkscrew pasta can be substituted for the rice.

❖❖❖

1   **cup uncooked rice**
¹/₄ **cup olive oil**
2   **tablespoons lemon juice**
³/₄ **teaspoon seasoned pepper**
¹/₂ **teaspoon salt**
¹/₂ **teaspoon rosemary**
¹/₂ **teaspoon oregano**
¹/₂ **teaspoon chopped garlic**
¹/₄ **teaspoon dried mint leaves**
1   **tomato, chopped**

❖❖❖

1. Cook rice according to package directions and while still hot, place in a bowl.
2. Mix oil, lemon juice and seasonings and add to rice.
3. Add chopped tomato and chill.

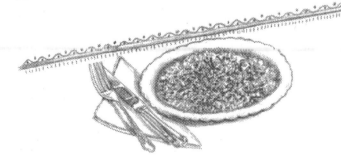

Kasha Salad

❖ **Notes** ❖

Our grandmothers would laugh to read an article I came across recently commenting that buckwheat groats —what Jews have always called kasha — was becoming the "in" thing for Washington hostesses to serve.

❖❖❖

1	**cup raw kasha**
1	**10-ounce package frozen peas, defrosted but not cooked**
$^1/_2$	**cup diced cucumber**
12	**cherry tomatoes, halved**
2	**tablespoons oil**
2	**tablespoons lemon juice**
$^1/_2$	**teaspoon powdered mustard**
$^1/_2$	**teaspoon curry powder**
$^1/_2$	**teaspoon garlic powder**
$^1/_8$	**teaspoon pepper**
$^1/_8$	**teaspoon paprika**

❖❖❖

1. Cook kasha according directions on package. Cool.
2. Add remaining ingredients.
3. Toss and serve.

Macaroni Salad

This recipe is one of my all-time favorites.

❖❖❖

8	ounces (2 cups) elbow macaroni
1/2	cup mayonnaise
1	tablespoon lemon juice
1	teaspoon salt
1	teaspoon sugar
1/4	teaspoon celery seed
1	tomato, diced
1	cup celery, diced
3	tablespoons chopped pimento
2	tablespoons chopped green pepper

❖❖❖

1. Cook macaroni as directed on package. Drain, rinse with cold water and drain again.
2. In a small bowl, mix mayonnaise with lemon juice, salt and sugar.
3. Combine with macaroni and add celery seed, tomato, celery, pimento and green pepper.

Potato Salad

❖ **Notes** ❖

Everyone has his or her favorite potato salad. This is my family's winner.

❖❖❖

5   medium potatoes (Red potatoes
    are best)
¹/₄ cup India or pickle relish
2   hard-boiled eggs, chopped
2   teaspoons prepared mustard
³/₄ cup mayonnaise
1   small onion, chopped fine
¹/₄ cup green olives, sliced or
    chopped
1¹/₂ teaspoons salt
¹/₈ teaspoon black pepper
    A dash of garlic powder
    Paprika for garnish

❖❖❖

1. Cook unpeeled potatoes until tender. Cool.
2. Peel and cut into cubes about ¹/₄ inch thick.
3. Mix all other ingredients together.
4. Chill. Garnish with paprika.

❖ For an interesting change, replace potatoes with lightly cooked cauliflower flowerettes. Delicious and different!

Belgian Endive and Watercress Salad

Both Belgian endives and watercress have become available in almost every supermarket. It makes a refreshingly different salad.

❖❖❖

2	bunches watercress
6	Belgian endives
2	tablespoons lemon juice, preferably fresh
6	tablespoons olive oil
1	teaspoon salt
$^1/_2$	teaspoon fresh ground pepper

❖❖❖

1. Trim stems from watercress and wash and dry thoroughly.
2. Trim root ends of endive and remove outer leaves if discolored.
3. Cut endive lengthwise into strips, wash and dry.
4. Place remaining ingredients together in a jar and shake thoroughly.
5. Just before serving, pour dressing over salad.

Donna's Broccoli Salad

❖ Notes ❖

My daughter manages to juggle a teaching job, six children, and putting some of the most creative meals on her table.

❖❖❖

1	bunch fresh broccoli
1	tablespoon sugar
	salt
$^1/_2$	cup broken cashews or 8–10 fresh mushrooms, chopped
$^1/_2$	cup mayonaise
2	cloves garlic, crushed
1	small jar sliced green olives
1	purple onion, chopped

❖❖❖

1. Break up or cut broccoli into florets. Drop into boiling salted water for $^1/_2$ a minute. Remove broccoli from water.
2. Pour water out and bring fresh water to a boil again. Drop broccoli into water again for $^1/_2$ a minute.
3. Mix with remaining ingredients.
4. Chill.

Chapter Ten

FISH

Fish is low in calories, low in fat, and pure simplicity to cook. It is irresistible from a nutritional point of view and (with certain exceptions) is very easy on the budget. You can make fish as casual or elegant as you wish. Most people who say they don't like fish have just never tasted well-prepared fish.

The most important thing to remember when buying fish is to buy only the freshest. Look for these signs:

1) Fresh fish smells clean; it does not smell fishy.
2) Whole fish should have shiny, bright skin.
3) The eyes should be bright (avoid fish with cloudy eyes).
4) The gills should be bright red or pink.
5) Fillets and steaks should be moist looking.
6) Frozen fish should be frozen solid and not appear freezer burned.

In general, you should allow 8 – 12 ounces of whole fish per serving, 6 – 8 ounces for fish steaks and 4 – 8 ounces for fillets.

Some examples of lean fish are: cod, flounder, grouper, haddock, hake, halibut, orange roughy, perch, pike, pollack, red snapper, sole and whiting.

Fattier kinds of fish contain more fish oil, which means more flavor, and more calories. Examples of fatty fish are: bluefish, butterfish, mackerel, sable, salmon, smelt, stripped bass and tuna.

Fish will dry out if you overcook it. Use the following Canadian Fisheries method for whole fish or fillets and you'll have perfectly cooked fish every time:

Place fish flat on plate or counter and measure its thickness — not length — with a ruler.

Cook fish 10 minutes for every inch thickness of fish. With very thin fillets of fish don't be afraid to cook them for only 3 – 4 minutes. They will be cooked.

If baked fish is dry and too firm, there's nothing you can do: it's been overcooked. As with most foods, it's better to check the fish as it cooks and put it back in again for another minute or two to finish cooking than to have a tough, overcooked piece of fish for dinner.

If you're going to keep the fish on a hot tray or reheat it, be sure to undercook it a little because it will cook further when reheated, and if already fully cooked, it will get dried out and tough.

If you have a microwave, by all means use it. Fish cooks very quickly by this method and retains its moisture. Usually microwave cooking time is 4 – 5 minutes for every pound of fish.

As a general rule of thumb, one type of fish can easily be substituted for another. It is best to substitute a fatty fish for another fatty fish, and a lean fish for a lean fish.

r Fish

Lemon-Garlic Fish Fillets

Parve
4 servings

❖❖❖

1–2 tablespoons olive oil
1   pound fish fillets
2   cloves garlic, chopped
     The juice of 1 lemon
$^1/_2$ teaspoon salt
     A dash of pepper

❖❖❖

1. Heat olive oil in large skillet over medium heat.
2. Add fish and garlic. Saute 10 minutes for every inch of thickness.
3. Add lemon juice, salt and pepper.
4. Cover and cook for another minute or two. Remove from skillet and serve.

❖ Notes ❖

Baked Nile Perch

❖ **Notes** ❖

Ridiculously simple to make.
Can be served as either a main course or appetizer.

❖❖❖

2   tablespoons olive oil
2   tablespoons soy sauce
2   teaspoons oriental sesame oil
1   large fillet of Nile perch, or any
       other large fish fillet
    **Garnish: sprigs of fresh basil
       or rosemary**

❖❖❖

1. Preheat oven to 350°.
2. Lay fish on a baking sheet and sprinkle 1 tablespoon olive oil onto each side of the fish.
3. Slowly and carefully (so as not to cut yourself on any remaining fish bones) rub the oil onto the fish until evenly distributed.
4. Do the same with the soy sauce. The fish should have a deep amber color.
5. Repeat with the sesame oil.
6. Bake 5 minutes for each $1/2$-inch thickness of fish.
7. Removed the fish from the oven when it is dark brown in color and flakes when tested with a fork.
8. Serve either hot or chilled.

❖ Don't confuse roasted oriental sesame oil, which has a strong flavor and aroma, with regular sesame oil which is light in color and mild in taste.

New Orleans Barbecued Fish

Parve
6 servings

I like to serve this with French bread to sop up the delicious juice.

❖❖❖

6	**fish fillets, cut into 1-inch strips**
3	**tablespoons parve margarine, melted**
3	**tablespoons olive oil**
1	**teaspoon paprika**
3	**tablespoons pickling spices**
$^1/_2$	**teaspoon oregano**
2	**teaspoons Worcestershire sauce**
4	**cloves garlic, minced**

❖❖❖

1. Melt margarine in saucepan.
2. Add remaining ingredients except fish and simmer for a minute or two.
3. Remove from heat, cool, and pour over fish.
4. Stir to coat fish and let marinate several hours or overnight in refrigerator.
5. Preheat oven to 400°.
6. Place fish and marinade in a baking pan and bake about 15 minutes.
7. Remove from pan and serve with juices.

Gefilte Fish

❖ **Notes** ❖

Although homemade gefilte fish tastes better than store-bought, it is not always cheaper to make (depending on your local prices). If budget is your main consideration and store-bought gefilte fish is on sale, consider buying that rather than making your own. If you do make your own, ask the fishmonger to save the heads and bones for the broth.

❖❖❖

6	pounds ground fish	1¹/₂	teaspoons pepper
7	onions	3	eggs
2	quarts water	³/₄	cup ice water
3	carrots, sliced	¹/₂	teaspoon sugar
4	teaspoons salt	3	tablespoons matzo meal

❖❖❖

❖ I prefer to use whitefish or a combination of whitefish and pike. If Nile perch is available it makes a delicious and very white gefilte fish.

❖ You can safely omit the matzo meal — the fish will still hold together if you beat it in a mixer, thoroughly, until it's very light and fluffy.

❖ The taste of gefilte fish is different depending on if it's served cold or warm. If you're not sure you like the taste of your sample ball, put it in the refrigerator or freezer to completely cool. Then taste it again.

1. Put fish heads and bones, 3 whole, peeled onions, 1 quart water, 2 teaspoons of the salt and ³/₄ teaspoon of the pepper in a large pot.
2. Cook over high heat while preparing fish.
3. In a food processor, chop remaining onions.
4. Add eggs, ice water, sugar, matzo meal, remaining salt and pepper and process until fluffy.
5. Add to fish mixture, mixing well.
   Test for taste:
6. Make a small ball of gefilte fish.
7. Place 1 cup of fish broth in a microwave-safe glass. Cook small ball of gefilte fish in the microwave for 5 minutes. When cool, taste. Adjust seasonings if necessary.

(Recipe Continued...)

Gefilte Fish... *(Recipe Continued...)*

8. Wet hands and shape fish mixture into patties or balls and carefully drop into fish stock.
9. Add carrots.
10. Cover pot loosely and cook over low heat for 1 hour.
11. Uncover pot and cook for another $1/2$ hour.
12. Cool before removing from water and refrigerate.

❖ **Notes** ❖

❖ The fish mixture can be shaped into logs to be sliced after cooking; or, you can freeze the uncooked logs until you're ready to cook and serve them. Don't defrost the logs — just cook them $1/2$ hour longer than the time recommended above.

Leftover Fish Casserole

Don't waste that leftover fish!

❖❖❖

2	8-ounce packages cream cheese
2	teaspoons milk
1	pound any cooked fish
4	teaspoons chopped onion
2	teaspoons red horseradish
$1/2$	teaspoon salt
	A dash of pepper
1	cup grated cheese

❖❖❖

1. Preheat oven to 350°.
2. Mix together all ingredients except cheese and place in greased casserole.
3. Sprinkle cheese on top and bake until warm and cheese is melted.

Parmesan Crusted Fish

Dairy
8 servings

❖ Notes ❖

❖❖❖

2   tablespoons grated Parmesan
       cheese
2   tablespoons prepared
       horseradish
2   tablespoons lemon juice
8   fish fillets
$^1/_2$ cup plain low-fat yogurt
2   tablespoons Dijon mustard
1   teaspoon margarine, melted
     vegetable cooking spray

❖❖❖

1. Combine 1 tablespoon grated Parmesan cheese, yogurt, horseradish, mustard, lemon juice and margarine.
2. Spread evenly on one side of fish.
3. Place fish, coated side up, on a rack coated with cooking spray; place rack in broiler pan.
4. Sprinkle with remaining Parmesan cheese.
5. Broil 6 inches from heat for 10 minutes, or until golden. Check for doneness after 6 – 7 minutes, depending on thickness of fish fillets. Fish should flake easily when tested with a fork.

Fish — Pizza Style

❖ **Notes** ❖

❖❖❖

1	pound fish fillets
2	tablespoons olive oil
1	medium onion, diced
2	tomatoes, diced; or 1 small can tomato sauce
$^1/_2$	teaspoon salt
	A dash of pepper
1	teaspoon basil
$^1/_2$	cup grated or shredded mozzarella cheese

❖❖❖

1. Heat olive oil in large skillet over medium heat.
2. Add onion and saute until golden but not brown.
3. Add tomatoes (or tomato sauce), salt and pepper, basil and fish fillets.
4. Saute 10 minutes for every inch of thickness of fish.
5. When fish is done, sprinkle with cheese.
6. Continue cooking just until cheese begins to melt.
7. Remove fish from pan and serve.

Salmon Florentine Pie

❖❖❖

2   tomatoes, sliced in ¹/₂ inch
      slices
1   7 ounce can salmon, drained
10 ounce package frozen spinach,
      thawed and drained
¹/₂ cup Pancake Mix or Biscuit Mix
2   eggs, beaten
      A pinch each of:
         garlic powder
         onion powder
         thyme
         dill
¹/₂ cup milk

❖❖❖

1. Preheat oven to 350°.
2. Oil an 8-inch pie pan, or spray with non-stick spray.
3. Arrange tomato slices in a layer covering bottom of pan.
4. Flake the salmon; distribute evenly over tomatoes.
5. Spread spinach over salmon.
6. Beat remaining ingredients together and pour over layers in pan.
7. Bake uncovered for 50 minutes or until set.
8. Let stand 5 minutes before cutting into wedges to serve.

❖ You can substitute equivalent amounts of canned tuna for the salmon, and/or chopped, thawed broccoli for the spinach.

Excellent Fish

Deliciously simple and simply delicious.

❖❖❖

2	pounds fish fillets or fish steaks
2	tablespoons bread crumbs
2	tablespoons olive oil
1	tablespoon lemon juice
3	tablespoons capers
1	tablespoon oregano
2	tablespoons minced onion
2	cups yogurt
	parsley flakes

❖❖❖

1. Preheat oven to 400°.
2. Place fish fillets or steaks in a shallow, greased baking pan.
3. Sprinkle with bread crumbs, oil, lemon juice, capers, oregano and minced onion.
4. Pour yogurt over fish and sprinkle with parsley flakes.
5. Bake for approximately 10 minutes, depending on thickness of fish, until fish flakes.

ABOUT FRIED FISH....

Fried fish is absolutely delightful when prepared properly. Follow these hints and your fried fish will turn out light and crispy every time.

1. Make sure the oil in the pan is hot enough. Test it with a small cube of bread. It should fry in 30 seconds.

2. Don't put too much fish in the pan at once. This will lower the temperature of the oil, and the fish, instead of frying in the oil will absorb it.

3. If the oil foams when you put in the fish, it means you haven't coated the fish well enough. Remove the fish and recoat it, first with flour, then with egg, and then again with flour, bread crumbs or matzo meal.

4. To drain excess oil after frying, lay the pieces of fish on top of crumpled paper towels. If you lay it on flat toweling, the fish will reabsorb the oil that has drained off.

5. If something goes wrong and your fish is soggy or limp after it's been fried, drain it and reheat the oil to a higher temperature. Then refry the fish until it becomes stiff and crisp.

Fried Fish with Lemon Butter

Dairy
8 servings

A nice dish to serve for a special weekday meal.

❖❖❖

2	**pounds fish fillets**
1	**teaspoon salt**
$^1/_8$	**teaspoon pepper**
1	**cup flour**
2	**eggs, beaten**
	Oil for frying
2	**tablespoons dry white wine**
2	**tablespoons lemon juice**
2	**tablespoons butter**
	Garnish: fresh parsley and lemon wedges

❖❖❖

1. Sprinkle fish with salt and pepper and dredge in flour.
2. Dip into beaten egg.
3. Pan fry in $^1/_2$ inch hot oil for 3 minutes, or until golden brown.
4. Turn and fry 2 more minutes.
5. Remove from pan and drain on crumpled paper towels.
6. Place on serving platter.
7. Melt butter, add lemon juice, and dry white wine.
8. Pour over fish and serve garnished with fresh parsley and lemon wedges.

Chapter Eleven
DAIRY AND EGG DISHES

Butter, eggs, cream and cheese have always had a special place in Jewish cooking. No Hanukkah is complete without potato latkes topped with sour cream; and Shavuot was just made for blintzes and cheesecake.

Dairy foods are usually inexpensive, and should be served regularly by the budget-conscious cook. If cholesterol is a problem, there are so many cholesterol-free dairy substitutes available, that the recipes in this section should pose no problem.

Blintz Casserole

May be served hot, warm or cold. It's wonderful topped with sour cream and/or cherry or blueberry pie filling.

❖❖❖

Dough:
1   cup butter, melted
$^1/_2$ cup sugar
2   eggs
1   cup flour
1   tablespoon baking powder
     A pinch of salt
$^1/_4$ cup milk
1   teaspoon vanilla

Filling:
2   pounds farmer cheese
     The juice of 1 lemon
$^1/_2$ cup sugar
2   eggs
     Salt to taste
4   ounce package cream cheese
1   teaspoon vanilla

❖❖❖

1. Combine all dough ingredients and mix well.
2. Spread half of dough on the bottom of a 2-quart casserole.
3. Mix filling ingredients together in a separate bowl and add to casserole.
4. Spread remaining dough on the top.
5. Bake 1$^1/_2$ hours at 300°, or until golden.

❖ If you want to freeze this casserole, underbake it so it doesn't dry out when you warm it up.

Boursin-Style Cheese

Dairy
3 cups

❖ **Notes** ❖

This delicious cheese is quite expensive to buy but so easy and inexpensive to make yourself. Serve this spread at room temperature with crackers.

❖❖❖

1	**cup butter, softened**
2	**8-ounce packages cream cheese, softened**
1	**clove garlic, minced**
$^1/_2$	**teaspoon each:**
	oregano
	pepper
$^1/_4$	**teaspoon each:**
	basil
	marjoram
	dill
	thyme

❖❖❖

1. Mix all ingredients together in a food processor or mixer until well blended.
2. Refrigerate overnight.
3. Serve at room temperature with crackers.

❖ Will keep for 2 to 4 weeks.

❖ Do not freeze.

Eggs in Purgatory

Dairy or Parve
6 servings

In Israel they serve a similar dish called shakshouka. This makes a good weeknight supper served with garlic bread.

❖❖❖

1 small can sliced mushrooms, drained	2 teaspoons oregano
	Salt and pepper to taste
8 tablespoons margarine	1 6-ounce can tomato paste (if necessary)
3 medium onions, chopped	
1 36-ounce can tomatoes, undrained	6 eggs
	A dash Tabasco or hot pepper sauce (optional)
2 teaspoons basil	

❖❖❖

1. In a large skillet, saute mushrooms in 2 tablespoons of the margarine until golden. Remove mushrooms.
2. Add another 2 tablespoons margarine and saute onions until soft.
3. Return mushrooms to skillet. Add undrained tomatoes, remaining 4 tablespoons of margarine, and spices. Simmer uncovered for 1 hour. If mixture is thin add tomato paste.
4. When ready to serve, place 6 cups of the tomato mixture in a skillet. Heat until edges begin to bubble.
5. Crack eggs and place in depressions made with spoon in tomato mixture.
6. Cover. Cook 4 – 5 minutes.
7. Remove eggs to plate with spatula and surround eggs with sauce.

❖ Sauce can be cooked the day before.

Farmer's Casserole

Dairy
2 servings

Delicious served with black bread and butter.

❖❖❖

2   cucumbers, finely chopped
4   radishes, finely chopped
2   tomatoes, finely chopped
4   green onions, finely chopped
1   small container cottage cheese
1   cup sour cream
$^1/_2$ teaspoon salt
$^1/_8$ teaspoon pepper

❖❖❖

Combine all ingredients and serve.

Easy Lasagna Squares

❖ **Notes** ❖

This takes only five minutes to prepare using our Homemade Biscuit Mix recipe.

❖❖❖

¹/₂	cup cottage cheese
¹/₄	cup grated Parmesan cheese
1	teaspoon oregano
¹/₂	teaspoon basil
1	6-ounce can tomato paste
2¹/₂	cups shredded mozzarella cheese
1	cup milk
2	eggs
²/₃	cup Homemade Biscuit Mix
	Salt and pepper to taste

❖❖❖

1. Preheat oven to 400°. Grease an 8-inch square baking dish.
2. Alternate layers of cottage cheese and Parmesan cheese in the baking dish.
3. In a separate bowl, mix herbs, tomato paste and ³/₄ cup of the mozzarella cheese; spoon evenly over top of cheese layer.
4. Beat together milk, eggs, Homemade Biscuit Mix, salt and pepper until smooth (about 1 minute).
5. Pour over cheese mixture in baking dish.
6. Bake until knife inserted in center comes out clean, approximately 30 minutes.
7. Sprinkle with remaining mozzarella cheese and serve.

Noodles Romanoff

Dairy
8–10 servings

A perfect side dish for a fish meal. I have been making this for over 30 years and it's always in demand.

❖❖❖

1   **pound fine noodles**
1   **16-ounce package cream**
      cheese
2$^1/_2$ **pints sour cream**
$^1/_4$ **cup onion, minced**
1   **teaspoon Worcestershire sauce**
$^1/_2$ **teaspoon garlic salt**
      A dash Tabasco or hot pepper
         sauce
1   **teaspoon salt**
$^1/_2$ **cup bread crumbs**
4   **tablespoons butter, melted**

❖❖❖

1. Cook noodles according to package directions and drain.
2. Combine cream cheese, sour cream, minced onion and seasonings.
3. Stir into cooked noodles.
4. Turn into greased 2-quart casserole, top with bread crumbs, drizzle with melted butter.
5. Bake in a 350° oven for 25 minutes.

Potato Cheese Kugel

❖ **Notes** ❖

Originally a Passover recipe this has become an all-year-round favorite — and there's never a crumb left over.

❖❖❖

6	eggs
4	cups water
2	6-ounce packages potato pancake mix
1¹/₂	cups sour cream
1	tablespoon parsley
2	pounds cottage cheese

❖❖❖

1. Combine eggs, water and potato pancake mix and let stand until thick.
2. Add remaining ingredients and pour into greased 9-inch pan.
3. Bake at 350° for 1 hour or until brown.

❖ Top each serving with a dollop of sour cream.

Vegetable Cheese Pie

Dairy

A great dish for a weeknight dinner. No specific amounts are given because it can be made with whatever ingredients and amounts you have on hand. Add a salad and you have a quick and tasty meal.

❖❖❖

Butter or margarine for sauteing
Onions, sliced
Mushrooms, sliced
Frozen puff pastry
Tomatoes, thinly sliced
Oregano or Italian seasoning
Cheese, grated or shredded

❖❖❖

1. Saute onions and mushrooms in butter or margarine.
2. Roll out puff pastry. Fit into bottom and sides of pie plate, or lay on a cookie sheet.
3. Add sauteed vegetables, oregano and top with sliced or shredded cheese and sliced tomatoes.
4. Bake in a 425° oven for 15 minutes, or until pastry puffs and turns golden, and cheese melts.

Impossibly Easy Pizza

Dairy
6 servings

❖ **Notes** ❖

Impossibly easy because it makes its own crust. You can add to or change the toppings to suit your taste.

❖❖❖

²/₃ cup plus ¹/₂ cup chopped onion
¹/₃ cup plus ¹/₄ cup grated
    Parmesan cheese
3 eggs
1¹/₂ cups milk
³/₄ cup Homemade Biscuit Mix
¹/₂ cup chopped green pepper
1¹/₂ cups shredded mozzarella
    cheese

Sauce:
1 6-ounce can tomato paste
¹/₄ cup water
1¹/₂ teaspoons oregano
¹/₂ teaspoon garlic salt
¹/₂ teaspoon basil
¹/₄ teaspoon pepper

❖❖❖

1. Preheat oven to 425°.
2. Grease a 10-inch pie plate and sprinkle with ²/₃ cup chopped onion and ¹/₃ cup grated Parmesan cheese.
3. In a food processor or blender beat eggs, milk and Homemade Biscuit Mix until smooth.
4. Pour over onions and cheese in pie plate.
5. Bake 20 minutes.
6. Mix sauce ingredients together and spread on pizza.
7. Layer remaining ¹/₄ cup Parmesan cheese, chopped green pepper and mozzarella cheese on top of pizza.
8. Bake for an additional 20 minutes, or until cheese is melted and lightly golden.

Cheese Casserole

Dairy
6 servings

Great for a busy day — put it together in the morning and pop it in the oven an hour before serving. A marvelous way to use up that leftover bread and cheese in your freezer.

❖❖❖

6–8 slices bread (remove crust)
Butter
2   cups grated cheese
2   cups milk
2   eggs
¹/₂   teaspoon salt
¹/₈   teaspoon pepper
¹/₂   teaspoon dry mustard

❖❖❖

1. Butter bread and place 3 slices in 8×8-inch casserole.
2. Cover with 1 cup grated cheese.
3. Repeat layers with remaining bread and cheese.
4. Mix remaining ingredients and beat until fluffy.
5. Pour over bread and cheese mixture; cover with plastic wrap and refrigerate overnight.
6. Remove from refrigerator 1 hour before baking and unwrap.
7. Bake 40 – 50 minutes in 350° oven.

Rich Noodle Pudding

Dairy
12 servings

Very rich and creamy.

❖❖❖

8	ounces noodles
½	cup milk
3	eggs
1	cup cottage cheese
1	cup sour cream
4	ounces cream cheese
4	ounces butter, melted
1	cup golden raisins
	pinch cinnamon

❖❖❖

1. Cook noodles according to manufacturer's direction. Drain.
2. Add remaining ingredients and mix well.
3. Pour into greased 9×13-inch pan.
4. Bake at 350° for 45 minutes.

Chapter Twelve
MEAT AND POULTRY

Many of our old, familiar notions about meat being the mainstay of a meal have been turned upside down. According to the Pyramid of Recommended Foods, meat should be served as a side dish rather than as a main course. This approach is not only healthy, it is also much easier on the budget!

Ground meat is the least expensive type of meat you can purchase. Next come chuck roasts, brisket, top flank, and neck meat. These cuts of meat are very flavorful, but tough, and require long, slow cooking.

The most expensive cuts of meat are rib roasts, rib steaks, and chops. These should be reserved for special occasions.

It makes good "budget sense" to buy a large roast when you find one on sale. You can use the meat to prepare several meals. For example, part of the roast can be served as barbecued beef or pot roast, another, smaller part can be made into stir-fry beef and you can use the leftovers to make pot pie.

If you don't have enough leftover meat to make another complete meal, save the meat in your freezer. When you have accumulated several packages — even different types of meat — they can be used together as a base for excellent casseroles or Chinese dishes.

THE CHOLENT STORY

Cholent (also called *chulent*, *shalet*, and *hamin*) deserves an explanation of its own. In fact, whole cookbooks have been written just on the subject of cholent!

The dish was originally invented to meet the need for a hot meal on Shabbat, when cooking is prohibited by Jewish law. As with chicken soup, almost every family has its own recipe for cholent that is "the *only* way to make it." Every cook has their own special formula for the correct type and amount of beans, barley and other ingredients. Some like their cholent with lots of liquid, some like it dry; some layer the ingredients, some mix them up. There are Ashkenazi, Sephardi and Hungarian versions of cholent, just to name a few.

Cholent can be as economical as you choose — and no one will know the difference! That's the beauty of cholent — it can be adapted to any budget or taste. Whatever the contents of the pot, it is the slow process of cooking (or baking) that makes cholent a delectable Shabbat dish.

Although many people consider cholent to be a side dish, I like to serve it as the main course. Sometimes I use a whole roast in the cholent, along with the other ingredients, to make a meal-in-a-pot. It's delicious served with cole slaw and a tossed salad.

Because cholent cooks slowly over a long period of time, it is the perfect recipe for the cheapest cut of meat available. If, however, I am going to serve the cholent as a side dish, or with several other dishes, I make a meatless cholent or one using leftover meat bits and gravy that I have frozen from a previous roast. Absolutely no flavor is lost and it helps out the budget considerably.

If you've never made cholent before, do take the plunge! Give it a try and you'll soon discover your own "only way to make cholent."

Cholent I

Meat

Marrow bones give a wonderful flavor to any cholent.

❖❖❖

2¹/₂ pounds of the cheapest cut of meat, cut into chunks	1 cup barley
2 pounds marrow bones	1 tablespoon salt
3 medium onions, coarsely chopped	1 teaspoon pepper
6 potatoes, scrubbed but not peeled	¹/₂ cup ketchup
3 sweet potatoes, scrubbed but not peeled	2 pounds stuffed kishka, whole
¹/₂ cup dry white beans, rinsed and checked	6 raw eggs in shell, well washed (optional)

❖❖❖

1. In an 8 quart pot or electric crockpot layer ingredients in order given.
2. Carefully fill the pot with water to about 2 inches above the ingredients.
3. Place the raw eggs in shell and kishka on top.
4. Cover pot tightly, bring to a boil, then reduce heat and cook on the lowest possible heat for at least 6 – 8 hours. (Cholent can also be baked in a 250° oven overnight.)
5. When ready to serve, remove the eggs carefully.
6. Remove kishka and cut into serving pieces. Place on top of serving bowl or platter of cholent, or serve separately with cooked eggs.

❖ Use meat if serving as a main course. If serving as a side dish, you may want to omit meat and add leftover meat gravy or 2 tablespoons beef flavored bouillon powder.

❖ If you spray your cholent pot with non-stick spray before you add the ingredients, it will make clean-up a snap.

❖ When making almost any kind of pot roast or brisket, you will generally have a good bit of meaty sauce or gravy left over, with bits of meat in it. Freeze this and use it later as a base for cholent. It will give your cholent an excellent flavor, and eliminate the need to actually add chunks of meat to the cholent.

Cholent II

Meat

This is a cholent with a special flavor because of the addition of prunes and burnt sugar.

❖❖❖

2	medium potatoes	2	tablespoons salt
1	pound dried lima beans	$^1/_2$	teaspoon pepper
4	large onions, finely chopped	2	small cut-up chickens
2	tablespoons oil		Kugel (see following recipe)
4 – 5	meat or marrow bones	2	tablespoons water
8 – 10	black prunes		
2	tablespoons sugar		

❖❖❖

1. Scrub potatoes.
2. Rinse and check beans.
3. Soak beans and potatoes separately in salted water for 2 hours.
4. In cholent pot or large casserole, saute onions in oil.
5. Add ingredients to the pot in layers in the following order: beans sprinkled with salt and pepper; marrow bones and chicken parts, sprinkled with salt and pepper; prunes; kugel and potatoes.
6. Place sugar in saucepan and cook over low heat until sugar is dark brown. (Watch carefully that it doesn't burn.) Remove from heat.
7. Add 2 tablespoons water, mix, and pour over layers in pot.
8. Add water to cover. If not using an electric crock pot, boil on high flame for 30 minutes, uncovered.
9. Cover and put in a 250° oven overnight.

Cholent Kugel

Meat

❖❖❖

3	onions, finely chopped
8	tablespoons oil
2	tablespoons parve margarine
1	cup self-rising flour
1	slice bread, soaked in water and squeezed dry
1	egg
2	tablespoons powdered chicken or beef bouillon
$^1/_2$	teaspoon salt
	A dash of pepper
1	cooking bag

❖❖❖

1. Saute onions in oil and margarine.
2. In a large bowl, put flour, fried onion (including oil), bread, egg, soup powder, salt and pepper.
3. Mix and knead dough. It should be fairly elastic. If necessary add a few teaspoonsful of water.
4. Put mixture into cooking bag and shape into a log. Punch a few holes with a fork at the tip of the bag. Add kugel to the cholent.
5. When serving the cholent, remove kugel from bag and serve separately, sliced.

Sweet & Sour Pot Roast

Meat
6–8 servings

❖❖❖

3	pounds chuck roast	2	tablespoons vinegar
2	tablespoons oil	1	tablespoon brown sugar
1	cup chopped onion	3/4	teaspoon salt
1	clove crushed garlic	1	bay leaf
3/4	cup hot water	1/4	cup flour
3	tablespoons ketchup	1/4	cup water

❖❖❖

1. Brown roast on all sides in hot oil in a Dutch oven; remove meat and set aside.
2. Saute onion and garlic in oil.
3. Return roast to pot and add next six ingredients. If pot handles are not ovenproof, cover with aluminum foil.
4. Cover and bake in a 325° oven for 3 hours or until tender.
5. Remove bay leaf and discard.
6. Remove roast from pot; slice and place on serving platter.
7. Measure liquid in pot.
8. For every cup of liquid mix together 2 tablespoons flour and 2 tablespoons cold water; blend well.
9. Stir flour and water mixture into hot liquid in pot, and cook over medium heat, stirring constantly until thickened.
10. Pour gravy over meat slices and serve.

Barbecued Beef

This dish goes a long way, and you're sure to have leftovers for another meal.

❖❖❖

4	pounds beef roast, cheapest cut
2	quarts water, or to cover
$^1/_2$	cup vinegar
1	large onion, chopped
$1^1/_2$	cups ketchup
$^1/_2$	cup brown sugar
1	teaspoon chopped garlic
2	tablespoons chopped onion
3	tablespoons liquid from meat
2	drops hot pepper sauce

❖❖❖

1. Cover meat with water in a large heavy pot on top of stove.
2. Add vinegar and onion and simmer 3 – 4 hours, until meat is very tender.
3. Place remaining ingredients in small saucepan and bring to a boil. Simmer sauce for 5 minutes and remove from heat.
4. When meat is cooked, let cool in juices, then remove from pot, saving liquid.
5. Shred meat (remove fat), and put in heavy oven-proof pan.
6. Bake meat in sauce in a 350° oven for 2 more hours, covered; or, in crock pot for 3 – 4 hours, or, in a covered disposable pan on the grill for 1 hour.
7. Freeze any remaining sauce for future use in cholent or casseroles.

Stew-Pot Beef

❖ Notes ❖

This recipe is an adaptation of a recipe from Julia Child. I like to serve it with noodles and a tossed salad.

❖❖❖

2 tablespoons olive oil	2 cups thinly sliced onions
1¹/₂ cups kosher white wine	3 pounds chuck roast, cut into 2-inch chunks
¹/₄ cup brandy or gin	1 teaspoon salt, or to taste
2 teaspoons salt	¹/₂ teaspoon pepper, or to taste
¹/₄ teaspoon pepper	1 cup flour, for dredging
¹/₂ teaspoon thyme or sage	4 firm, ripe tomatoes, chopped
1 bay leaf	1¹/₂ cups fresh mushrooms, sliced
2 cloves garlic, minced	
2 cups thinly sliced carrots	

❖❖❖

1. Mix together olive oil, wine, brandy, salt, pepper, thyme, bay leaf, garlic, carrots and onions in a large plastic bag.
2. Add meat chunks and marinate for at least six hours or overnight.
3. Remove meat from marinade, and scrape off marinade.
4. Season meat lightly with salt and pepper, dredge in flour and set aside.
5. Drain marinade liquid into a bowl. Toss in tomatoes and mushrooms to marinade.
6. In a 6-quart fireproof casserole, layer meat and mixed vegetables, ending with a top layer of vegetables.
7. Pour in marinade liquid.

(Recipe Continued...)

Stew-Pot Beef... *(Recipe Continued...)*

8. Cover casserole, and simmer for about 15 minutes on the stovetop. If vegetables haven't yielded enough liquid to almost cover the meat, add a little bouillon.
9. Continue simmering until meat is tender, about 2 hours.
10. Taste for seasoning.
11. In a separate small bowl, mix cold water with flour until smooth.
12. Add 1 tablespoon liquid to 2 tablespoons of flour and return to casserole. Boil a minute or two until liquid is thickened.

❖ **Notes** ❖

❖ To "dress-up" and enhance this dish for guests:
1. Finely chop 2 cloves of garlic and place in a bowl with 3 tablespoons drained capers.
2. Thoroughly stir in 3 tablespoons of Dijon-type mustard.
3. Gradually beat in 3 tablespoons of olive oil to make a thick sauce.
4. Stir in $1/4$ cup minced fresh basil or parsley, and add sauce to the finished Stew-Pot Beef just before serving.

Beverly's Brisket

I used this recipe in several of my cooking classes and many years later former students told me that this was still their favorite brisket recipe.

❖❖❖

5 pounds brisket of beef	1 large onion, thinly sliced
2 teaspoons salt	3 ribs celery, cut into strips lengthwise
$3/4$ teaspoon pepper	$1 1/2$ cups boiling water
$1/2$ teaspoon paprika	1 beef bouillon cube
$1/2$ teaspoon garlic salt	1 (29-ounce) can tomato sauce
$1/2$ teaspoon onion salt	$1/4$ cup browning sauce (optional)
$1/2$ teaspoon dry mustard	$1/2$ cup peach or apricot preserves
3 medium carrots, peeled and cut into strips lengthwise	

❖❖❖

1. Preheat oven to 500°.
2. Wash and pat dry brisket. Sprinkle both sides with spices.
3. Place meat in a roasting pan, fat side down and bake in preheated oven until brown, about $1/2$ hour.
4. Remove meat from oven; lower temperature to 350°.
5. Drain fat, then add carrots, onion and celery to meat.
6. Dissolve bouillon cube in boiling water and pour over roast.
7. Add tomato sauce, browning sauce and preserves.
8. Cook, basting often until tender (approximately 45 minutes per pound).
9. Remove from oven, allow to cool, and slice against the grain.
10. Reheat before serving, adding more water if necessary.

❖ This recipe is best made the day before serving.

Chili Mac

Meat
20 servings

Ground meat is not only the least expensive, but also the most versatile meat you can serve. This recipe will feed a small army and it freezes well. Serve with salad and French bread.

❖❖❖

¹/₄ cup plus 2 tablespoons olive oil	1 teaspoon hot pepper sauce
6 medium onions, chopped	¹/₄ cup plus 2 tablespoons chili powder
3 cloves garlic, chopped	
3 pounds ground beef	4 15-ounce cans kidney beans
1 20-ounce can tomatoes, drained (save liquid)	2 cups reserved liquid from tomatoes and beans
1 16-ounce can tomato paste	1 pound vermicelli pasta
1 29-ounce can tomato sauce	A pinch of salt
1 tablespoon salt	

❖❖❖

1. Pour ¹/₄ cup oil into a large pot and heat.
2. Add onions and garlic and saute until onion is limp.
3. Add ground beef and brown, stirring occasionally.
4. When meat is browned, drain off excess fat.
5. Add tomatoes, tomato paste, tomato sauce, salt, pepper sauce and chili powder.
6. Simmer 1 hour.
7. Add beans and cook until thick.
8. Use reserved liquid from the tomatoes and beans to thin chili if necessary.
9. Cook pasta in a large pot of water to which 2 tablespoons of olive oil and salt have been added.
10. Drain pasta, rinse with cold water and drain well.
11. Mix pasta with chili and bake in a 350° oven for approximately 30 minutes.

Hamburger Helper

Quick and easy to prepare. The kids will clamor for more.

❖❖❖

1	pound ground meat
1	teaspoon salt or to taste
1/4	teaspoon pepper or to taste
1	teaspoon garlic powder
	A dash of Tabasco sauce (optional)
6	cups water
1	pound noodles, uncooked
1/4	cup flour
1/2	cup water

❖❖❖

1. Brown the meat in a 6-quart pot.
2. Add salt and pepper, garlic powder, Tabasco (optional) and water and bring to a boil.
3. Add noodles.
4. Cook until noodles are tender, about 10 minutes.
5. Mix flour with 1/2 cup cold water; add to mixture and stir constantly until thickened.

❖ **Notes** ❖

❖ Leftover vegetables can be added if desired.

❖ This dish can also be made with leftover boneless meat. Simply place meat in pot, add salt and pepper and continue as above.

Hot Tamale Pie

Meat
6 servings

❖❖❖

1/2	cup chopped onion	1	6-ounce can tomato paste
2	cloves garlic, chopped	1 1/2	cups corn meal
1	pound ground beef	4	tablespoons flour
1	tablespoon oil	1	teaspoon chili powder
3	tablespoons plus 1 teaspoon chili powder	2	teaspoons salt
1/2	teaspoon black pepper	1 1/2	cups cold water
		2	cups boiling water

❖❖❖

1. Brown onions, garlic and beef in oil.
2. Add 3 tablespoons chili powder, pepper and tomato paste.
3. Cover and simmer 15 minutes.
4. Remove from heat and set aside.
5. In a saucepan, mix corn meal, flour, 1 teaspoon chili powder and salt.
6. Add 1 1/2 cups *cold* water and mix.
7. Stir in 2 cups boiling water.
8. Cook on low flame, stirring constantly until thick.
9. Cover and continue cooking over low heat 10 minutes longer, stirring occasionally.
10. Spread 1/2 of cornmeal mush on bottom of greased 9-inch pie plate.
11. Add meat filling and top with remainder of mush.
12. Bake in a 375° oven for 30 minutes.

❖ In most recipes, ground beef, veal, turkey, and chicken are interchangeable. However, veal, turkey and chicken are blander in flavor than beef so, if you use them instead of beef in a recipe, increase the seasonings accordingly.

Meatloaf in Puff Pastry

Meat
8 servings

This takes ground beef from ordinary to elegant. Delicious hot or cold.

❖❖❖

1	pound ground beef	1	teaspoon salt
1	pound ground chicken or turkey	¹/₂	teaspoon pepper
4	cloves garlic, minced	2	tablespoons mustard
1	onion, finely chopped	1	8×10-inch sheet puff pastry, defrosted
2	cups matzo meal or bread crumbs	1	egg, beaten

❖❖❖

1. Mix ground beef with half of chopped garlic, half of chopped onion, 1 cup matzo meal or bread crumbs, and salt and pepper.
2. Grease a sheet of aluminum foil. Spread ground beef on foil to form a flat rectangle.
3. In a separate bowl, mix ground chicken or turkey with remaining garlic powder, matzo meal, salt and pepper, and mustard.
4. Cover ground beef rectangle with chicken mixture.
5. Roll up jelly roll fashion, leaving foil behind.
6. Place thawed puff pastry on flat surface; place meat roll on puff pastry.
7. Roll and cover meat mixture in pastry; trim and seal edges with water.
8. Brush with beaten egg.
9. Bake in a 350° oven for half an hour, covered with foil.
10. Uncover and bake for an additional half hour or until done.

About Chicken...

It is only possible to cut one chicken into so many pieces. However, chicken recipes *can* be stretched. Here are a number of excellent ways to make your chicken go further:

Choose the right recipe. Grilling or frying your chicken is the most expensive way to serve it. Most people can eat several pieces, so you'll need to serve a good amount. If you have unexpected company coming and not enough chicken on hand, use a recipe that has a rich sauce, such as Chicken Superlative. Not only is it a delicious dish, but because it is so rich most people will be satisfied with only one piece.

Leg quarters (legs and thighs) are generally the least expensive parts to buy other than wings and backs. However, if your family eats only breasts and you're not inclined to use the other parts as suggested, you're better off buying just the parts that they do eat.

Check prices in your area. In some areas there is no price difference between buying a whole or a cut-up chicken. Check local prices so you know what is most economical for your needs.

Cut the chicken into smaller pieces. Cut your bird into eighths, or have the butcher do it. If you are serving children, you might want to have the chicken cut into sixteenths.

Make complete (and creative) use of breast meat. Debone the breast and use either as whole boneless breasts or cut into bite-size pieces to use as chicken nuggets.

Use everything. Save bones and necks in a separate bag in the freezer to use for soup. Save wings separately to use in Chicken Fricassee or Glazed Chicken Wings.

Although buying boneless chicken breasts is the most expensive way to buy chicken, if you are making a dish such as stir-fry, where two or three chicken breasts will serve six people, it becomes less expensive and more worthwhile to use boneless chicken breast.

Glazed Chicken Wings

Meat
8 servings

Children love chicken wings and they make an inexpensive meal. Adults will love these too. They'll disappear so quickly you'll wish you had made more.

❖❖❖

8 pairs of chicken wings (about 3 pounds)	1 12-ounce jar apricot preserves
1 teaspoon salt	$^1/_3$ cup prepared mustard
$^1/_8$ teaspoon pepper	$^1/_4$ cup brown sugar, packed
Flour	$^1/_2$ teaspoon salt
$^1/_2$ cup parve margarine	$^1/_4$ teaspoon pepper
10$^1/_2$ ounces strong beef broth or bouillon	2 cups rice, cooked
	Canned cling-peach slices (optional)
	Whole, peeled apricots (optional)

❖❖❖

1. Sprinkle chicken wings with salt, pepper and flour.
2. Saute wings in $^1/_2$ cup margarine until very well browned on all sides.
3. Add undiluted can of broth, then cover and continue cooking until largest wing is fork-tender.
4. Meanwhile, in a small saucepan over low heat, stir together apricot preserves, mustard, and brown sugar, $^1/_2$ teaspoon salt and $^1/_4$ teaspoon pepper until bubbly.
5. Line a large cookie sheet with foil (to make cleanup easier).
6. Preheat broiler for 10 minutes.
7. Place chicken wings on foil-lined cookie sheet and brush liberally with glaze.
8. Broil until bubbly and well browned.
9. Turn the wings, brush again with glaze, then broil again.
10. Pile cooked rice in the center of a platter and surround with chicken wings.
11. Surround with peach slices and pile whole apricots on top of rice (optional).
12. Place remaining glaze in a bowl, and serve alongside the rice and wings.

Baked Chicken Epstein

Meat
4–6 servings

This has been a standard in my house for many, many years.

❖❖❖

1	**chicken, cut up**
2	**tablespoons powdered chicken bouillon**
¹/₂	**teaspoon garlic powder**
¹/₂	**teaspoon onion powder**
1	**teaspoon seasoned salt**
1	**teaspoon dill**
	A dash of lemon juice

❖❖❖

1. Place chicken pieces skin side up in a baking pan.
2. Sprinkle with seasoning and add 1 – 2 cups water.
3. Bake in a 400° oven for 1 hour or until skin is crisp and chicken is done. Additional water may be added as necessary to keep the chicken from sticking to the pan; however, don't let chicken cook in the water.

Chicken Drumstick Crown

Meat
6 servings

❖ **Notes** ❖

Crown Roast of Lamb is one of the most elegant —and expensive — dishes created. This delicious chicken version looks lovely and you'll blush from the compliments you receive.

❖❖❖

$1/2$ **cup flour**	1 **can (8$1/2$-ounce) pineapple slices**
1 **teaspoon salt**	2 **cups white rice, cooked**
$1/4$ **teaspoon pepper**	1 **ripe avocado**
2 **teaspoons paprika**	2 **tablespoons lemon juice**
12 **chicken drumsticks**	$1/2$ **pound seedless red grapes**
$1/2$ **cup parve margarine**	

❖❖❖

1. In a bowl or a plastic bag combine flour, salt, pepper and paprika. Coat drumsticks on all sides with this mixture.

2. Saute flour-coated drumsticks in a large skillet in melted margarine until golden brown on all sides.

3. Add pineapple syrup from canned pineapple. Cover the skillet and simmer drumsticks about 30 minutes, or until tender.

4. Peel avocado; cut in half crosswise, remove pit, then slice into six slices $3/4$-inch thick; cut them in half.

5. Brush the slices with the lemon juice.

6. Rinse the grapes, then separate them.

7. Cut 6 pineapple slices in half.

8. When drumsticks are tender, mound rice in center of serving plate. Place drumsticks in circle, standing up against rice.

9. Arrange a pineapple and avocado slice under every drumstick. Garnish with a few grapes between drumsticks.

Chicken Puff Pastry Roll

Meat

Shortly before Passover, I went through my freezer trying to use things up. I had a roll of puff pastry dough, a container of soup chicken (including the vegetables), and half a package of instant mashed potatoes. This is the dish I made for Shabbat and my guests loved it. One of them even told me she made it the following Shabbat for her company!

You'll notice there are no exact amounts specified. That's because this recipe is so flexible you can just put it together with any items and amounts you have on hand.

❖❖❖

	Soup chicken and vegetables	1	roll frozen puff pastry, defrosted
2	eggs plus 1 yolk		Approximately 4 cups mashed
2	tablespoons mustard		potatoes

❖❖❖

1. Mix deboned soup chicken and vegetables with mustard. Taste for seasoning.
2. Add any other seasoning that strikes your fancy.
3. Add beaten eggs and set aside.
4. Unroll defrosted puff pastry.
5. Cut into thirds if you're using a large roll.
6. Spread puff pastry with mashed potatoes, then a layer of chicken and vegetable mixture.
7. Roll up firmly and place seam-side down on a greased baking tray lined with foil.
8. Brush with beaten egg yolk and prick with a fork to allow steam to escape.
9. Bake, uncovered, in a 400° oven until pastry is puffed and golden.

Chicken Fricassee

Makes an excellent appetizer or main course.

❖❖❖

	Necks, gizzards and wings from 3 or more chickens	2	teaspoons salt, or to taste
2	large onions, sliced	$^1/_2$	teaspoon pepper, or to taste
3	stalks celery, sliced	2	tablespoons ketchup
1	pound ground meat	2	tablespoons bread crumbs
1	egg	2	tablespoons dark brown sugar
		1	tablespoon lemon juice

❖❖❖

1. Clean gizzards, cut wings in half.
2. Place chicken necks, gizzards and wings in a large saucepan and cover with water to which 1 teaspoon salt has been added.
3. Add sliced onions and celery and cook, covered, for $1^1/_2$ hours on low heat.
4. Remove from heat.
5. Mash the onion and celery into the broth to thicken.
6. Mix ground meat with egg, 1 teaspoon salt, pepper, ketchup and bread crumbs.
7. Form into balls and drop into chicken broth mixture.
8. Add brown sugar, lemon juice and more water if necessary. Taste for sweet-sour flavor and simmer until gizzards are tender, about 1 hour.

Barbecued Chicken

Meat
6 servings

To make this recipe even quicker and simpler, use bottled barbecue sauce. A delicious rerun for leftover chicken or turkey.

❖❖❖

1	cup ketchup
¹/₂	cup chopped onion
4	tablespoons brown sugar
2	tablespoons mustard
2	cloves garlic, chopped
1	chicken cut into eighths

❖❖❖

1. Cook all ingredients except chicken for about 5 minutes.
2. Pour over chicken and bake, uncovered, in a 350° oven for 1 hour or until chicken is tender.

❖ If using cooked chicken or turkey, pour barbecue sauce over chicken and bake until heated through.

Quick Chicken Pot Pie

Meat
6–8 Servings

A great way to use up your soup chicken. Any other leftover chicken or meat can be substituted.

❖❖❖

3 cups cooked chicken, cubed, shredded or coarsely chopped	**¹/₂** teaspoon garlic powder
1¹/₂ cups chicken broth or bouillon	**1** onion, coarsely chopped
2 tablespoons flour	**1** teaspoon salt
1 10-ounce package frozen peas and carrots, defrosted	**¹/₈** teaspoon pepper
	1 8×10-inch sheet frozen puff pastry

❖❖❖

1. Preheat oven to 450°.
2. Mix flour with 3 tablespoons of cold water and place in saucepan.
3. Add remaining ingredients and cook until thick and bubbly.
4. Place in 2-quart casserole.
5. Cover with puff pastry dough which has been rolled out to ¹/₂ inch wider than casserole.
6. Seal with water and prick holes in top for steam to escape.
7. Bake for 10 minutes or until pastry is puffed and golden.

❖ **Notes** ❖

❖ If substituting meat for chicken, substitute beef broth or bouillon

❖ A layer of cooked mashed potatoes may also be substituted for the top crust.

Lemon-Garlic Chicken

Meat
6 servings

Another winning way to use up leftover chicken. I like to serve this with fresh string beans and rice.

❖❖❖

1	tablespoon olive oil
4	cups boneless cooked chicken or 6 raw boneless chicken breasts
4	cloves garlic, chopped
	Juice of 1 lemon
1	teaspoon salt
¹/₈	teaspoon pepper

❖❖❖

1. Heat olive oil in large skillet over medium heat.
2. Add cooked chicken and garlic and saute 2 – 3 minutes.
3. Add lemon juice, salt and pepper, cover and cook for another minute or two, just until chicken is heated through. Remove from skillet and serve.

❖ If using raw chicken breasts, saute about 8 minutes or until chicken is browned and cooked through.

"Glop" Salad

For some unremembered reason my daughters nicknamed this dish "Glop Salad", and so it has remained! Though the name isn't elegant, it can be a lovely dish to serve for guests, especially for a summer lunch. It's so simple to make that it's almost embarrassing when people ask for the recipe...and they invariably do.

❖❖❖

1	large package frozen mixed vegetables (broccoli, cauliflower, carrots, baby corn, etc.)
1	8-ounce package tri-color pasta
4	cups boneless cooked chicken or meat (leftover grilled chicken or meat is especially good), cubed or shredded
$^3/_4$	cup Oriental salad dressing

❖❖❖

1. Defrost frozen vegetables but don't cook.
2. Cook pasta according to package directions. Drain and place in large bowl.
3. Add defrosted vegetables and meat.
4. Add salad dressing, toss and serve.

❖ This dish can be extended by adding additional pasta.

❖ The ingredients can be mixed and/or matched to suit your taste and seasonal availability.

Chicken Superlative

Meat
6 servings

I served this dish at a $100-a-plate benefit dinner and it was a great hit. It is also an excellent budget stretcher because, wonderful as it is, it's so rich that people will rarely eat more than one piece of chicken.

❖❖❖

$^1/_3$ **cup flour**
$^1/_4$ **teaspoon salt**
$^1/_8$ **teaspoon pepper**
3   **tablespoons parve margarine**
1   **chicken, cut up**
1   **envelope onion soup mix**
$^1/_2$ **cup water**
$^1/_4$ **cup dry white wine**
1   **tablespoon lemon juice**
$^1/_4$ **teaspoon thyme**
1   **clove garlic, minced**

❖❖❖

1. Preheat oven to 350°.
2. Combine flour, salt and pepper in a plastic bag. Shake chicken pieces in it to coat.
3. In a large skillet, melt margarine and brown chicken pieces on both sides; remove to casserole.
4. In a bowl combine soup mix, water, wine, lemon juice, thyme and garlic. Pour over chicken.
5. Cover and bake 45 minutes. Uncover and bake 15 minutes more.

❖ **Notes** ❖

❖ For hors d'oeuvres or for a buffet, use chicken drumettes, boneless chicken breasts or cut-up boneless chicken breasts.

Chicken Marengo

❖ **Notes** ❖

This dish is based on one I was served many years ago at the British Colonial Hotel in Nassau. The addition of the green olives gives it an unusual twist. It's excellent served with plain white rice.

❖❖❖

3 tablespoons olive oil	1 8-ounce can tomatoes or 1^1/$_2$ cups diced fresh tomatoes
1 chicken, cup up	
1^1/$_2$ teaspoons salt	2 tablespoons flour
^{1}/$_4$ teaspoon ground black pepper	1 cup dry white wine
^{3}/$_4$ cup chopped onions	1^1/$_2$ cups chicken broth
1 clove garlic, minced or	^{1}/$_2$ pound fresh mushrooms, sliced
^{1}/$_4$ teaspoon garlic powder	^{1}/$_2$ cup green olives, optional

❖❖❖

1. Heat oil in large skillet.
2. Brown the chicken in hot oil.
3. Add the salt, pepper, onions and garlic and saute for a minute or two.
4. Add tomatoes.
5. Sprinkle with flour and gradually mix in the wine and broth.
6. Cover and cook over low heat until chicken is tender (about 30 – 45 minutes).
7. Saute the mushrooms in margarine until lightly golden.
8. Add mushrooms and olives to the chicken and cook for 15 minutes longer.
9. Taste for seasoning.

Chapter Thirteen
VEGETABLES AND SIDE DISHES

Vegetables make a valuable contribution to any menu. They are full of nutrition, flavor, color and texture. Properly chosen and prepared, vegetable dishes will give appetizing variety to any meal.

In America, we are fortunate to be able to purchase almost any kind of vegetable all year round. But the best way to economize is to buy vegetables when they are in season. Produce that is in season is not only less expensive, it's fresher and healthier too.

Another smart way to economize is to buy Grade B vegetables. Of course, if you are serving sliced tomatoes or steamed broccoli, you will want to buy the best quality produce available. But, there are other times — when you're making a soup or casserole — when you can use Grade B vegetables with no compromise in taste or quality. You can save money and no one will know the difference.

Be careful, though, and don't confuse Grade B with over-ripe or rotted produce. Grade B is generally produce that, except for defects in size or shape, or slight soft spots, is just like Grade A.

If you live near a farmer's market, take advantage of your good fortune. I used to live near the DeKalb County Farmer's Market in Atlanta and very often, at the end of the week in the late afternoon, perfectly good produce would be drastically reduced in price because it would not keep until the beginning of the next week. There were even times when I was offered a case of lovely produce for free!

Remember, vegetables when overcooked are neither appetizing nor nutritious. Always cook vegetables for less time than you think they need. It's much easier to cook them for an extra minute, if need be, than it is to turn back the clock on overcooked vegetables.

If you do overcook a vegetable so that it's unpleasantly soft and mushy, puree it with a little margarine, salt and pepper and serve it as though that's the way it was meant to be.

Spinach Italian Style

Parve
8 servings

❖❖❖

2	pounds fresh spinach, washed
1	clove garlic, minced
3	tablespoons olive oil
1	6-ounce can tomato paste
1	teaspoon salt
$^1/_4$	teaspoon pepper

❖❖❖

1. Cook spinach until tender in boiling water.
2. Drain and chop fine.
3. Brown garlic in oil.
4. Add spinach and tomato paste.
5. Cook 15 minutes and add salt and pepper.

Spinach Oriental

Parve
4 servings

❖❖❖

1	pound fresh spinach
2	tablespoons oil or parve margarine
1	teaspoon grated onion
2	tablespoons sesame seeds
2	tablespoons soy sauce

❖❖❖

1. Wash spinach well. Drain and remove tough stems.
2. In a skillet, heat the oil or margarine.
3. Add onion and sesame seeds and saute over medium heat, stirring constantly, until the seeds are browned.
4. Add drained spinach and soy sauce.
5. Cover and cook about 5 minutes or until tender.

Asparagus

Though plentiful and inexpensive for a brief period in the spring, asparagus is very expensive the rest of the year — if it's even available. When this unique vegetable is properly selected and prepared, the memory of its taste will carry you through to the following asparagus season.

Select thick stalks that are firm and fresh looking, with closed tips. Look for spears that are mostly green. Asparagus should be cooked and served the day it is purchased. If you are not going to serve it within a day or two, blanch and freeze them.

Asparagus I   *Dairy or Parve*

1. Melt 2 tablespoons of butter or margarine in a large frying pan and add asparagus spears.
2. Cover and cook over medium heat, shaking pan occasionally, for 3 – 5 minutes, depending on the size of the stalks.
3. Check for doneness by tasting one stalk, or by breaking it. It should be crunchy-tender, not soft.
4. If it is still too crisp, continue to cook for a few more minutes. It's better to err on the short side of cooking time before testing for doneness.

Asparagus II   *Parve*

You can also simmer asparagus for 3 – 5 minutes as above in 2 inches of water instead of butter; or, steam them in a vegetable steamer over boiling water.

❖ **Notes** ❖

❖ To prepare asparagus: Wash in running water; then soak for a few minutes in salted water (especially the tips). Drain, and rinse again. Snap off the white, woody ends of the spears and save them to flavor a soup. Peel each stalk with a vegetable peeler.

❖ If you plan to keep asparagus on a hot tray or to reheat it, reduce cooking time. Otherwise it will be overcooked and mushy when reheated.

❖ Asparagus is superb served with hollandaise sauce, or simply a squeeze of lemon juice and salt and pepper.

Veggie Bake

❖❖❖

1	10-ounce package frozen cauliflower
2	10-ounce packages frozen peas and carrots
1$^1/_2$ cups sour cream	
1	tablespoon minced onion
1	teaspoon salt
3	tablespoons dry bread crumbs
1	medium tomato, sliced

❖❖❖

1. Cook vegetables according to package directions. Be careful not to overcook. Drain well.
2. Combine vegetables, sour cream, onion and salt. Stir gently until combined.
3. Place in 1$^1/_2$-quart casserole, sprinkle with bread crumbs and arrange tomato slices on top.
4. Bake for 20 minutes in a 325° oven or until bubbly.

Barley Casserole

❖ **Notes** ❖

A nice change of pace from rice and potatoes.

❖❖❖

¹/₂ **pound fresh mushrooms, sliced**
4   **tablespoons oil or parve**
      margarine
2   **medium onions, chopped**
1   **cup barley**
1   **teaspoon salt**
¹/₄ **teaspoon pepper**
2¹/₂ **cups parve beef or chicken**
      bouillon

❖❖❖

1. Heat oil in frying pan.
2. Add chopped onions and cook about 5 minutes.
3. Add mushrooms and cook another 3 minutes.
4. Add barley and brown lightly, mixing well with onions and mushrooms. Season to taste with salt and pepper.
5. Pour into greased casserole and add enough broth to cover mixture and come ¹/₂ inch above it.
6. Cover tightly and bake in a 350° oven, for 25 minutes.
7. Taste barley for doneness and add more bouillon if necessary. Continue cooking until liquid is absorbed and barley is tender.

Broccoli Kugel

❖ **Notes** ❖

Cauliflower or chopped spinach can be substituted for the broccoli.

❖❖❖

3	ten-ounce packages frozen chopped broccoli
1¹/₂	tablespoons oil
1¹/₂	tablespoons flour
¹/₂	cup cream or parve cream
¹/₂	cup mayonnaise
1	tablespoon onion soup mix
3	eggs, well beaten
1	teaspoon salt
¹/₄	teaspoon pepper
1	tablespoon parve chicken bouillon powder, or 1 cube
1	cup cornflake crumbs

❖❖❖

1. Cook and drain broccoli. Set aside.
2. In a saucepan heat oil, add flour and cook gently until thick.
3. Add cream, mayonnaise, onion soup mix, well-beaten eggs, and salt and pepper to taste. Stir to blend ingredients.
4. Add drained broccoli and pour mixture into a greased 9×9-inch baking dish which has been coated with cornflake crumbs.
5. Top with additional crumbs and bake until firm to touch in a 350° oven for approximately 45 minutes.

❖ This kugel can be frozen.

Crusty Potato Cake

Parve
8 servings

Served in one large cake, it has a crisp golden-brown crust and translucent tenderness inside.

❖❖❖

6	large potatoes, peeled	¹/₄	teaspoon pepper
1	large onion, thinly sliced	2	tablespoons parve margarine,
3	tablespoons oil		softened (optional)
1	tablespoon salt		

❖❖❖

1. Using a food processor with a thin slicing disk, slice potatoes very thin.
2. Place sliced potatoes in cold water to cover for about ¹/₂ hour. This prevents discoloration.
3. Rinse potatoes thoroughly under running water, drain, and dry thoroughly on kitchen towels.
4. Heat 2 tablespoons of the oil in a heavy frying pan (preferably one with a non-stick finish) over medium heat, until oil begins to ripple. (If frying pan does not have non-stick finish, use 4 tablespoons of oil.)
5. Add drained potato slices and onions and saute, shaking the pan and turning potatoes frequently, until they are lightly browned and beginning to soften, about 10 minutes.
6. Season with salt and pepper and press potatoes down with a spatula.
7. Continue cooking and shaking the pan frequently to prevent sticking, until the bottom is golden brown, about 7–10 minutes.
8. Invert potato cake onto a lightly oiled large flat plate so that the browned side faces up. If the frying pan is dry, add remaining tablespoon oil at this point.
9. Slide cake back into the frying pan and cook until potatoes are tender and the second side is golden brown, about 7–10 minutes.

Hungarian Cabbage and Noodle Casserole

Parve
10 servings

Don't turn your nose up at this dish — one taste and you'll be hooked!

❖❖❖

3	tablespoons oil
2	large onions, sliced
1	medium-sized head cabbage, shredded
1	teaspoon salt
$1/4$	teaspoon pepper
2	packages (16-ounces each) broad noodles
1	tablespoon prepared mustard

❖❖❖

1. Heat oil in a large pot.
2. Saute onions in oil until well browned but not burnt.
3. Add shredded cabbage and salt and cook until soft.
4. Cook noodles according to package directions. Add to cabbage and onions and mix well.
5. Add mustard and mix well. Serve.

Glazed Baby Carrots

Parve
8 servings

❖❖❖

1   **bag frozen baby carrots**
2   **tablespoons parve margarine**
1   **teaspoon lemon juice**
$^1/_3$ **cup apricot or peach jam**
     Water

❖❖❖

1. Cook carrots in 1 inch of boiling salted water in a covered pan until they are just tender, or microwave for 3 – 4 minutes.
2. Drain.
3. Melt margarine in large frying pan.
4. Transfer carrots to frying pan with melted margarine.
5. Add lemon juice and jam; stir to glaze as sauce becomes hot.

Grilled Potatoes and Onions

Parve or Meat

This will be a welcome addition to whatever you're cooking on the grill.

❖❖❖

1   **potato per person**
1   **onion per person**
1   **teaspoon seasoned salt**
1   **tablespoon parve margarine per potato**
     Paprika

❖❖❖

1. Slice potatoes and onions.
2. Place in 8×8-inch foil pan or on double thickness of aluminum foil.
3. Sprinkle with seasoned salt and paprika.
4. Dot with margarine, seal and cook on grill while you're grilling the main course.

Amy's Potato Kugel/Latkes

Parve
6 servings

My daughter Amy always makes two kugels at a time, one for dinner... and the other to eat as a snack, straight out of the oven. She insists that the kugel tastes better if you grate the potatoes and onions by hand — and her kugel is always outstanding.

❖❖❖

$^1/_3$	cup oil
6	medium potatoes, peeled
2	onions
6	eggs, beaten
1	tablespoon salt
$^1/_2$	teaspoon pepper

❖❖❖

1. Preheat oven to 350°.
2. Pour oil into 8×8-inch Pyrex casserole or heavy ovenproof pan and heat in oven.
3. Meanwhile, grate potatoes and onions.
4. Add eggs and salt and mix well.
5. Add the hot oil and stir immediately.
6. Pour batter back into Pyrex dish, dust with pepper and bake for approximately 2 hours or until top is brown and crusty.

❖ Use same batter for latkes. Drop by tablespoonful into hot oil and fry on both sides until crisp.

❖ Potatoes absorb a lot of salt. This kugel tastes best when it's a bit on the salty side, so feel free to experiment and add more salt if needed.

Applesauce Noodle Kugel

❖ **Notes** ❖

❖❖❖

1	8-ounce package medium-wide noodles
¹/₂	pound cottage cheese
¹/₂	pint sour cream
1	cup applesauce
3	eggs, well beaten
1	teaspoon salt
¹/₄	cup butter or margarine

❖❖❖

1. Cook noodles according to package directions; drain and rinse in cold water.
2. Combine the remaining ingredients.
3. Pour into greased casserole and bake in a 350° oven for 45 minutes.
4. Increase oven temperature to 400° and bake an additional 15 minutes until kugel is crisp and brown.

Rice Kugel

Parve
8 servings

This simple dish can serve as a side dish, or even a dessert.

❖❖❖

2   **cups raw rice**
8   **eggs**
2   **cups apple or orange juice**
1¹/₂ **cups sugar**
2   **tablespoons oil**
1   **teaspoon cinnamon**
2   **teaspoons vanilla**
¹/₂   **cup raisins**

❖❖❖

1. Cook rice, drain, and combine with remaining ingredients.
2. Pour into 10×12-inch greased baking pan and bake for 1 hour at 350°.

Israeli Rice

❖❖❖

2   medium onions, finely chopped
¹/₃ cup plus one tablespoon olive
     oil
2   cups raw rice
1¹/₂ teaspoons curry powder
1   teaspoon salt
4   cups parve chicken bouillon
¹/₂ cup chopped nuts

❖❖❖

1. Saute onions in oil until soft but not brown.
2. Add rice, curry powder, salt, bouillon. Cover and cook on low heat until rice is tender but not overly soft.
3. Saute the nuts in 1 tablespoon oil until lightly browned. Add to the rice.

Spiced Orange Rice

Parve
4–6 servings

Rice cooked in orange juice with ginger and cinnamon makes a deliciously different dish.

❖❖❖

2	tablespoons oil
1	medium onion, diced
1	cup rice
2^1/$_2$	cups orange juice
1	teaspoon salt
^{1}/$_8$	teaspoon ginger
^{1}/$_8$	teaspoon cinnamon

❖❖❖

1. Heat oil in a medum saucepan and saute the onion until limp.
2. Add the rice and stir briefly to coat all the grains with oil.
3. Stir in the orange juice and seasonings.
4. Bring to a boil and simmer, covered, over low heat, for 25 minutes or until liquid is absorbed.

Lemon Vegetables

❖ **Notes** ❖

❖❖❖

4	small new potatoes, unpeeled and sliced
2	yellow squash, cut into thin strips
$^1/_3$	cup margarine, melted
2	tablespoons fresh lemon juice
$^1/_4$	teaspoon salt
2	carrots, cut into thin strips
1	zucchini, sliced
1	tablespoon grated lemon rind
$^1/_6$	teaspoon pepper

❖❖❖

1. Arrange potatoes and carrots in a vegetable steamer over boiling water, cover and steam 8 minutes or microwave vegetables in 1 tablespoon water for 2–3 minutes.
2. Add yellow squash and zucchini; cover and steam another 2 minutes, or until crisp-tender.
3. Place vegetables in serving bowl. Combine margarine and remaining ingredients.
4. Pour mixture over vegetables, tossing gently.

❖ If keeping vegetables warm on warming tray or reheating, undercook them so they don't get mushy.

Applesauce Loaf

Parve
1 loaf

Can be served as a side dish or dessert.

❖❖❖

$^1/_2$ cup shortening	$^1/_2$ teaspoon nutmeg
1 cup sugar	$^1/_4$ teaspoon allspice
1 egg, beaten	$^1/_4$ teaspoon cloves
$1^2/_3$ cups flour plus $^1/_3$ cup flour	1 cup applesauce
1 teaspoon baking soda	1 cup chopped pecans or walnuts
$^1/_2$ teaspoon salt	1 cup raisins
1 teaspoon cinnamon	$^1/_4$ cup plus 1 tablespoon wine

❖❖❖

1. Line a 9×5×3-inch loaf pan with waxed paper, grease and set aside.
2. Cream shortening in mixer, add sugar and beat until creamy.
3. Add egg and mix well.
4. In a separate bowl combine $1^2/_3$ cups flour, baking soda, salt and spices.
5. Add this and the applesauce to the creamed mixture, alternating between the two, beginning and ending with the flour mixture.
6. Dredge pecans and raisins in remaining $^1/_3$ cup flour to coat them well and fold into batter.
7. Spoon into prepared loaf pan.
8. Bake in a 350° oven for 1 hour and 15 minutes or until done.
9. Cool 10 minutes in pan, then remove from pan and cool completely on a rack.
10. Wrap in aluminum foil and refrigerate. May be served warm or cold.

Roasted Garlic

Parve

Garlic has always been known as a health-promoting food.

My grandmother used to eat a clove of garlic every day when she was a child in Russia. Today, many people take garlic pills for the same reason.

Roasted garlic is absolutely delicious! (Even if it is healthy.) Plus, you can eat a lot of it and no one will ever know.

❖❖❖

6   **heads of garlic**
2   **teaspoons olive oil for each bulb**

❖❖❖

1. Preheat oven to 350°.
2. Remove the outer layer of skin from garlic bulbs.
3. Cut $\frac{1}{2}$ inch off from each bulb straight across top.
4. Arrange in shallow baking pan.
5. Drizzle olive oil over each bulb, letting it run between the cloves.
6. Cover garlic with foil and bake 30 minutes.
7. Remove foil and bake 30 minutes more, or until garlic is tender when pierced with a toothpick.
8. Cool slightly.
9. To serve, squeeze the roasted garlic from each clove onto toasted rounds of bread or vegetables.

❖ To remove the smell of garlic from your hands rinse them in cold water, then rub with tomato juice or salt. Wash with soap and water.

Tsimmes

Parve
8 servings

❖❖❖

1	**pound prunes**
¹/₂	**pound dried apricots**
1	**teaspoon cinnamon**
1	**tablespoon lemon juice**
1	**onion, chopped**
1	**tablespoon oil**
1	**tablespoon cornstarch**

❖❖❖

1. Cook prunes and apricots in water to cover with cinnamon and lemon juice until tender.
2. Saute onion in oil until browned.
3. Add to fruit.
4. Drain fruit, reserving 1¹/₂ cups liquid.
5. Mix 1 tablespoon cold water with cornstarch and stir into fruit liquid.
6. Return liquid to fruit and cook on medium heat, stirring constantly, until thickened.

Donna's Vegetable Quiche

❖ **Notes** ❖

You can use any vegetable or combination of vegetables you choose for this kugel.

❖❖❖

2	**cups shredded zucchini**
4	**tablespoons flour**
4	**tablespoons mayonnaise**
2	**tablespoons onion soup mix**
2	**eggs**
	Sliced tomatoes

❖❖❖

1. Squeeze water from shredded zucchini.
2. Add remaining ingredients except tomatoes.
3. Place in 8-inch square greased baking pan.
4. Decorate top of kugel with very thin slices of tomato.
5. Bake in a 350° oven for 45 minutes.

❖ This recipe doubles easily.
Use a 9×13-inch pan.

Garden Fresh Pasta Salad

Dairy
6 servings

This recipe for cooked, mixed vegetables with cheddar cheese and pasta won the National Pasta Recipe contest many years ago, and is still a winner.

❖❖❖

7	ounces macaroni, cooked, drained, rinsed and drained again
1	10-ounce package frozen mixed vegetables, cooked and drained
1	cup diced cheddar cheese
1	cup mayonnaise
1	teaspooon salt
$^1/_4$	teaspoon onion powder
$^1/_2$	teaspoon pepper
	Lettuce leaves (optional)

❖❖❖

1. In a large mixing bowl, gently but thoroughly combine all the ingredients.
2. Chill. Serve on lettuce leaves if desired.

Vegetable Pancakes

❖ **Notes** ❖

Delicious served with salsa.

❖❖❖

1	**16-ounce package frozen corn, thawed**
$^1/_2$	**cup chopped green onions**
1	**medium onion, chopped**
2	**teaspoons oil**
2	**mashed potatoes**
$^1/_2$	**cup flour**
2	**eggs**
1	**teaspoon salt**
$^1/_2$	**teaspoon pepper**
2	**tablespoons or more margarine**

❖❖❖

1. Saute corn, green onions and onion in oil in large frying pan, stirring constantly for 2 minutes. Remove from heat.
2. In a separate bowl, combine mashed potatoes, flour and eggs.
3. Stir in corn mixture, salt and pepper.
4. Melt 1 tablespoon margarine in frying pan.
5. Drop mixture by tablespoons into frying pan.
6. Cook pancakes 2 minutes on each side until golden.
7. Add 1 tablespoon margarine, if needed.

Pasta with Garlic, Oil and Anchovies

Parve
6 servings

If you don't care for anchovies, omit them. It's still a very tasty and pretty dish.

❖❖❖

1	**pound spaghetti or other pasta**
3	**cloves garlic, peeled**
¹/₂	**cup olive oil**
1	**2-ounce can anchovies**
2	**tablespoons chopped fresh parsley**

❖❖❖

1. Cook spaghetti according to package directions.
2. While spaghetti is cooking, brown garlic in a small skillet in olive oil. Discard garlic.
3. Stir in anchovies, crushing them with back of spoon or a potato masher.
4. Add the parsley, stir, and remove skillet from heat.
5. Drain cooked spaghetti, add sauce and mix.

Potato Hash

Dairy or Parve

This Polish favorite is delicious, inexpensive and easy to prepare. For a quick every-day meal serve with a salad. Also great for Passover.

❖❖❖

1	potato per person
1	medium onion per person
	Oil for sauteing
1	teaspoon salt
¹/₄	teaspoon pepper
1	tablespoon butter or margarine per person
2	eggs per person

❖❖❖

1. Peel onions and potatoes and cut into thin slices or dice.
2. In a skillet, saute in butter or margarine until onions are browned and potatoes are cooked and slightly browned.
3. Add salt and pepper.
4. Divide potato mixture onto plates.
5. Fry eggs, sunny side up, and place on top of potato hash.

Chapter Fourteen
DESSERT

Desserts can be irresistible, gorgeous and downright mouth-wateringly delicious without breaking your budget. Consider the type of meal the dessert is going to follow. For instance, if you serve a heavy meat meal, think of simple fruit desserts like Poached Vanilla Pears or Strawberries in Fresh Orange Juice. Or, if you do decide to follow a rich meal with a rich dessert, plan on serving very small portions.

Sometimes I choose the dessert I want to make and plan the meal around it. Remember, you can always balance the cost of an expensive main course with an inexpensive yet elegant dessert such as Dacquoise au Chocolat.

Arlene's Cheesecake

❖ **Notes** ❖

My cousin Arlene Strauss's cheesecake is the first one I ever made over 30 years ago, and it's still my first chioce.

❖❖❖

18	**graham crackers or petit beurre crackers**
1	**cup sugar**
4	**eggs**
1	**cup sour cream**
¹/₂	**cup melted butter**
2¹/₂	**pounds farmers cheese or 4 8 ounce cream cheese**
1	**teaspoon vanilla**
2	**tablespoons sugar**

❖❖❖

1. Crush graham crackers into crumbs and mix with melted butter. Press onto bottom of 9×13 inch pan and bake for 5 minutes at 325°.
2. Cream cheese in mixer and gradually add sugar, eggs and vanilla.
3. Pour into pan and bake at 325° for 30 minutes.
4. Mix 2 tablespoons sugar with sour cream and spread over cake. Bake for 5 minutes at 500°.
5. Cool and refrigerate. Freezes well.

Devil's Food Cake

Parve
16 servings

This is not only delicious but very quick and simple to make. If you have a large mixer, double the recipe and have one to serve and one to freeze.

❖❖❖

1	cup cocoa
2¹/₂	cups sugar
2	teaspoons vanilla
2¹/₂	cups flour
1	teaspoon baking soda
2	cups hot water
5	eggs
1	cup oil
¹/₂	teaspoon salt
1¹/₂	teaspoons baking powder

❖❖❖

1. Combine all ingredients together in mixer. Beat for 3 minutes on medium speed.
2. Pour into 10×14-inch baking pan which has been either greased and floured or lined with waxed paper.
3. Bake at 350° for 1 hour.

Banana Split Dessert

Dairy or Parve
16 servings

❖❖❖

First layer:
2   cups cookie crumbs
$^1/_2$ cup melted margarine
2   tablespoons powdered sugar

1. Mix and spread in a 9×13-inch baking pan.

Second layer:
$^1/_2$ cup margarine
1   pound powdered sugar
3   egg whites

2. Cream margarine and sugar, add egg whites and beat until light and fluffy.
3. Spread over first layer in pan.

Third layer:
4-5 sliced bananas
1   large can crushed pineapple

4. Drain pineapple, combine with sliced bananas and layer in pan.

Fourth layer:
2   cups parve whipping cream,
      whipped
   **Garnish: cherries, peanuts
      and/or chocolate bits**

5. Generously spread pan with whipped topping and garnish with cherries, peanuts and/or chocolate bits. May also be drizzled with chocolate syrup.
6. Refrigerate or freeze until ready to serve.

❖❖❖

Pineapple Split Cake

Dairy
10–12 servings

A quick and lovely cake that can be used for Passover if you use a passover cake for the base.

1	prepared cake, sponge, pound, or white
1	1-pound jar apricot preserves
2	cups ice cream or whipped topping
3	ripe bananas, sliced
1	can pineapple slices

❖❖❖

1. Slice cake horizontally into two layers.
2. On attractive serving plate, arrange one layer of cake.
3. In small saucepan, melt apricot jam. Spread some jam over cake layer.
4. Spread with layer of ice cream or whipped topping, top with banana slices and another layer of cake.
5. Arrange pineapple slices attractively on top of cake and then spread with jam to form glaze.
6. Refrigerate or freeze until ready to serve.

Berry Bread Pudding

Parve
8 servings

An excellent way to use up leftover challah and other breads.

❖❖❖

8	slices challah or any other stale bread
⅓	cup parve margarine
4	cups berries, any kind
1	cup sugar
1	teaspoon cinnamon

❖❖❖

1. Spread margarine on one side of challah slices.
2. Place four slices of the challah, buttered side up, in a greased 9×9-inch baking dish.
3. Spoon 2 cups of berries on top.
4. Mix cinnamon and sugar and sprinkle half of it over berries. Mash berries with a potato masher so that berry juice seeps into the challah.
5. Arrange remaining challah slices, buttered side up over crushed berries and sugar/cinnamon mixture. Mash again.
6. Bake in a preheated 350° oven for 45 minutes.
7. Mash pudding again with potato masher and bake for an additional 20 minutes, or until bubbly and syrupy.
8. Cool slightly before serving. May be topped with parve ice cream or whipped cream.

❖ Make this in the summertime when lucious fresh blueberries and other berries are plentiful and inexpensive.

Pecan-Praline Bread Pudding

Dairy or Parve
12 servings

❖❖❖

1   tablespoon margarine, softened
1/2 cup raisins
1/4 cup bourbon
6   cups French bread or challah,
        cut into 1/2 inch cubes
4   cups half-and-half or parve
        cream
6   eggs
1/2 cup sugar

1   tablespoon vanilla
1/4 teaspoon salt
1/8 teaspoon ground nutmeg

Pecan-Praline Topping

2   tablespoons margarine
1/2 cup packed brown sugar
1/3 heavy cream or parve cream
1/2 cup pecans, coarsely chopped and
        toasted

❖❖❖

1. Preheat oven to 350°. Butter a 2 1/2-quart baking dish and set aside.

2. In a small bowl, mix raisins and bourbon.

3. In a large bowl, mix bread and half and half; let soak 10 minutes.

4. In medium bowl, beat eggs, sugar, vanilla, salt and nutmeg to mix.

5. Stir in raisin and egg mixtures into bread mixture; mix. Spoon into prepared dish.

6. Bake 45 – 50 minutes until pudding is puffed, top is brown and knife inserted 1 inch from edge comes out clean.

7. Cool on rack 30 minutes.

8. Meanwhile make topping:

9. In saucepan, over medium heat, stir margarine and brown sugar until margarine melts.

10. Add cream and mix.

11. Cook until sugar dissolves and mixture thickens. Add pecans.

12. Pour into bowl; cool 15 minutes. Drizzle over pudding and serve warm.

Almond Pudding Cake

❖❖❖

1$^1/_3$ cups toasted and finely
     chopped almonds
2$^1/_2$ cups Biscuit Mix (See Bread
     section for recipe)
$^1/_4$ cup sugar
1   package (3$^3/_4$ ounces) vanilla
     instant pudding mix
$^2/_3$ cup water
$^1/_4$ cup oil
4   eggs

❖❖❖

1. Preheat oven to 350°.
2. Generously grease 9×5×3-inch loaf pan. Press $^1/_3$ cup of almonds onto bottom and sides.
3. Mix remaining ingredients in large mixer bowl on medium speed for 3 minutes, scraping bowl occasionally.
4. Pour into ungreased pan and bake 50 minutes or until toothpick comes out clean. Remove from pan immediately and cool on wire rack.
5. Spread with creamy glaze (see following recipe) and garnish with whole almonds.

Creamy Glaze

Parve

❖❖❖

1   cup powdered sugar
1   teaspoon almond or vanilla
      extract
1–2 tablespoons water

❖❖❖

Beat until smooth and creamy.

Dacquoise au Chocolat

Dairy or Parve
10 servings

This chocolate meringue and nut cake is easier to make than it appears at first glance. It is easy on the budget and makes a spectacular appearance when you want to impress guests.
You will need a pastry bag and tube. Do not try to make meringues on a damp or rainy day — they won't dry out properly.

❖❖❖

$^3/_4$ **cup sugar**
$1^1/_4$ **cups nuts, browned in oven and ground**
1 **tablespoon cornstarch**
A dash of salt
6 **egg whites**

2 **tablespoons powdered sugar**
$1^1/_2$ **cups whipping cream (parve or diary)**
1 **tablespoon rum or brandy**
Chocolate Butter Cream (see following page)

❖❖❖

1. Preheat oven to 350°.
2. Coat two cookie sheets with non-stick spray or margarine and flour. (To do this, grease cookie sheet with margarine, then dust with flour and shake off excess flour). With your finger, mark off a 10-inch circle on each cookie sheet.
3. Mix together sugar, nuts and cornstarch.
4. Whip egg whites and a dash of salt in an electric mixer. Beat until firm.
5. Fold in the sugar and nut mixture. Work fast to prevent the whites from becoming grainy.
6. Fill a pastry bag fitted with a plain tube with the meringue mixture. Pipe a ring on each tray, following the outline of the 10-inch ring.
7. Divide the remaining meringue between the two rings and spread evenly with a spatula. The discs should be the same thickness all over.
8. Bake for 20 minutes until browned. Let the discs sit for a few minutes, then slide off tray to a wire cooling rack. Meringues will become dry and brittle after about 30 minutes.

(Recipe continued...)

Dacquoise... *(Recipe continued...)*

9. Handling carefully, trim edges if necessary to have perfect discs. Save the scraps.
10. Make Chocolate Butter Cream.
11. Place one disk on a serving platter and, using a pastry bag fitted with a fluted tube, pipe a border of chocolate butter cream all around the edge of the disc. Place a small amount of the butter cream in the middle of the disc and sprinkle with the scraps from the disc.
12. Combine the whipping cream, powdered sugar and rum. Whip until stiff.
13. Arrange the whipped cream in the middle of the disc. Place the other disc, smooth side up, on top.
14. Sprinkle with powdered sugar, coating the entire top.
15. Decorate the edges and middle with remaining chocolate butter cream.
16. Refrigerate until ready to serve. Use a serrated knife to cut.

❖ Notes ❖

Chocolate Butter Cream

A wonderfully rich butter cream.

3 ounces chocolate (1 semisweet, 2 bitter)
$^1/_3$ cup sugar
$^1/_4$ cup water
3 egg yolks
$^1/_2$ pound margarine, softened

1. Melt chocolate in microwave or in top of double boiler. Set aside.
2. Mix sugar and water in a saucepan and boil for 2 minutes.
3. Place yolks in a mixer or food processor bowl and pour sugar syrup on top of yolks, mixing on medium speed.
4. Increase mixer speed to high and continue beating for another 5 minutes until mixture is pale yellow and thick.
5. With mixer at low to medium speed add margarine, bit by bit, until the cream is smooth.
6. Add the melted chocolate and beat well.

Brownie Mix

Parve
16–17 cups

❖❖❖

6	cups flour
4	teaspoons baking powder
4	teaspoons salt
8	cups sugar
1	cup unsweetened cocoa
2	cups vegetable shortening

❖❖❖

1. Blend dry ingredients together and cut in shortening with two knives, a pastry blender, or your fingers, until mixture resembles cornmeal.
2. Place in an airtight container. Use within three months.

Chewy Brownies

❖❖❖

2	eggs
1	teaspoon vanilla
1¹/₂	cups Brownie Mix
¹/₂	cup chopped nuts (optional)

❖❖❖

1. Spray an 8-inch square pan with non-stick baking spray.
2. Combine first three ingredients in a food processor bowl or medium sized bowl and beat until smooth.
3. Add nuts if desired.
4. Back in a 350° oven for about 30 minutes, or until edges separate from the sides of the pan.

❖ For cake-like brownies add 2 tablespoons of water to the batter before beating.

Mississippi Mud

Dairy or Parve
16 servings

❖❖❖

4	eggs	1	teaspoon vanilla
¹/₂	cup melted margarine	1	cup flaked coconut
3	cups Brownie Mix	1	7-ounce jar marshmallow creme

❖❖❖

1. Spray a 9×13-inch baking pan with non-stick baking spray.
2. Beat eggs until foamy in the large bowl of a mixer.
3. Add melted margarine and mix well.
4. Add Brownie Mix, vanilla and coconut. Mix well.
5. Pour into prepared pan and bake in a 350° oven for 30 minutes, or until edges separate from the sides of the pan.
6. Remove from oven and cool.
7. Spread cake with marshmallow creme. Frost with chocolate icing.

Chocolate Icing

❖❖❖

¹/₂ cup margarine
6 tablespoons water
4 tablespoons unsweetened cocoa powder
Powdered sugar

❖❖❖

1. Mix together all ingredients except the powdered sugar in a saucepan. Bring to a boil, stirring constantly.
2. Remove from heat and immediately add powdered sugar.
3. Beat icing until smooth. Cool before frosting cake.

Cookie Crumb Crust Mix

❖ **Notes** ❖

This is a great mix to have on hand. Use it in any recipe calling for a cookie crumb crust.

❖❖❖

6   cups flour
1¹/₂ cups chopped nuts
1¹/₂ cups brown sugar, firmly
        packed
1   pound margarine, softened

❖❖❖

1. Combine flour, nuts and brown sugar and blend well.
2. With two knives, a pastry blender or your fingers, cut in margarine until mixture resembles cornmeal.
3. Press mixture firmly into two ungreased baking pans.
4. Bake in a 375° oven for 15 minutes. Cool.
5. Crumble and place in an airtight container. If not using within 4 – 6 weeks, store in freezer.

Cookie Crumb Pie Crust

Dairy or Parve

❖❖❖

$1^1/_3$ **cups Cookie Crumb Mix**
$^1/_2$ **teaspoon vanilla or almond flavoring**
$^1/_3$ **cup melted margarine**

❖❖❖

1. Preheat oven to 375°.
2. Combine all ingredients and stir to moisten.
3. Press evenly over bottom and up sides of 9-inch pie pan.
4. Bake for 8 minutes. Cool on wire rack before filling.

To Microwave:
1. Use same ingredients and amounts.
2. Put margarine in microwave-safe pie plate and microwave on medium for 45 seconds, until melted.
3. Add remaining ingredients and mix in pie plate with fork or rubber spatula until well blended and moistened.
4. Press firmly and evenly over bottom and up sides of pie plate.
5. Microwave on medium for $2 - 2^1/_2$ minutes, until crust has set. Be sure to rotate the pie plate a half turn after one minute. Cool completely before filling.

Roulade

The French call them roulades. Our grandmothers called them jelly rolls. They were — and still are — a quick and inexpensive dessert. Whether simple or elegant, a Jelly Roll is always dramatic to serve. Fill it however you like: with jelly, seasonal fresh fruits, ice cream, whipped cream mixtures, cake fillings or frostings — your imagination is the only limit.

❖❖❖

4 eggs, room temperature	1 teaspoon vanilla
$3/4$ teaspoon baking powder	$3/4$ cup flour
1 teaspoon salt	Powdered sugar
$3/4$ cup sugar	

❖❖❖

1. Preheat oven to 400°.
2. Line a greased $15^1/_2 \times 10^1/_2$-inch jelly roll pan with parchment paper and grease again.
3. Beat the eggs together with the baking powder and salt until very thick and lemon colored.
4. Gradually beat in the sugar. The mixture will form a ribbon as it drops from the beaters, when lifted.
5. Gently fold the vanilla into the egg mixture. Pour batter into jelly roll pan and spread evenly.
6. Bake for about 10 minutes, or until lightly browned. Cake is done when it barely begins to turn golden and top springs back if pressed with finger. Do not overbake or it will break apart when rolled.
7. Remove from oven and sprinkle top of jelly roll with a thin layer of powdered sugar. Cover with a sheet of waxed paper.
8. Rinse and wring out a kitchen towel and lay it over the waxed paper. Turn cake upside down and immediately roll it up in the damp towel. Cake can be rolled up from either the short or long end, depending on whether you want a long or a fat roll.
9. Let cool for 15 minutes. Unroll, remove waxed paper, fill and reroll. The jelly roll may now be wrapped in foil and a plastic bag and frozen, if you wish.
10. To serve, transfer roll to a platter and sprinkle with powdered sugar. Decorate with strawberries, whipped cream, a fresh flower or a sprig of ivy.

❖ Jelly Rolls freeze beautifully.

❖ If using a fresh flower or ivy sprig, be sure to wash it first.

❖ Variations:
  1. Fill roll with whipped cream and cover with chocolate mousse.
  2. Fill with your favorite jam or jelly.
  3. Fill with your favorite ice cream and freeze. Serve plain or top with hot fudge sauce or drizzled with chocolate syrup.

French Apple Pie

Dairy or Parve
8 servings

Makes it's own crust as it bakes.

❖❖❖

6 cups peeled, sliced tart apples	**Streusel:**
1 ¼ teaspoons cinnamon	1 cup biscuit mix
¼ teaspoon ground nutmeg	½ cup chopped nuts
1 cup sugar	⅓ cup brown sugar, firmly
¾ cup apple juice	packed
½ cup Biscuit Mix (see Bread section for recipe)	3 tablespoons margarine
2 eggs	
2 tablespoons margarine, softened	

❖❖❖

1. Preheat oven to 325°.
2. Mix apples and spices, and place in a 10-inch pie plate.
3. Process sugar, juice, Biscuit Mix, eggs and margarine in a blender or food processor until smooth. Pour over apples in pie plate.
4. Mix streusel ingredients until crumbly and sprinkle over pie.
5. Bake for about an hour or until knife inserted in center comes out clean.

Carrot Cake

Parve
16 servings

There are more recipes for carrot cake than I can count and I've probably tried them all — but I always come back to this one. It's so rich and delicious it doesn't need icing. But, if you prefer, you can sprinkle it with powdered sugar just before serving.

❖❖❖

2	cups flour
1	teaspoon salt
2	cups sugar
2	teaspoons cinnamon
2	teaspoons baking soda
1 1/2	cups oil
4	eggs
3	cups grated carrots

❖❖❖

1. Mix dry ingredients together.
2. Add oil and eggs and mix well.
3. Add carrots and mix.
4. Pour into greased tube or bundt pan.
5. Bake 50 minutes at 350°, or until cake leaves sides of pan.
6. Let cool 5 minutes and then run knife around edges. Turn out onto cooling rack.

Hot Fudge Pudding Cake

Dairy or Parve
10 servings

Hot, rich, and delicious!

❖❖❖

2	cups flour
4	teaspoons baking powder
$^1/_2$	teaspoon salt
$1^1/_2$	cups sugar
$^1/_3$	cup plus $^1/_2$ cup unsweetened cocoa
2	cups pecans or walnuts, chopped
1	cup water
4	tablespoons margarine, melted
2	cups brown sugar
$3^1/_2$	cups boiling water

❖❖❖

1. Preheat oven to 350°.
2. Sift together flour, baking powder, salt, sugar and $^1/_3$ cup cocoa. Stir in the water, margarine and nuts. The batter will be very thick.
3. Spread batter in a 9×13-inch baking dish.
4. Mix brown sugar with $^1/_2$ cup cocoa and sprinkle over batter.
5. Place pan in oven and then pour boiling water over the batter. Bake for 45 minutes. Bubbles will appear around the edges. The top will be firm but will "float." Serve warm.

Donna's Hamantashen

Parve
24 Hamantashen

Every year I try new Hamantashen recipes and always come back to my daughter's recipe.

❖❖❖

¹/₃ **cup oil**
¹/₂ **cup sugar**
¹/₄ **cup honey**
1   **tablespoon lemon juice**
2   **eggs**
2¹/₂ **cups flour**
2¹/₂ **teaspoons baking powder**
¹/₄ **teaspoon salt**
     Any thick jam (except for cherry,
        which is too runny)

❖❖❖

1. Mix oil, sugar, honey, eggs and lemon juice.
2. Add flour, baking powder and salt. Mix until thoroughly blended.
3. Roll out dough ¹/₄-inch thick; cut circles with a glass or cookie-cutter.
4. Fill circles with 1 teaspoon jam or other filling and bring edges together in center to form a triangle.
5. Bake 20 minutes in a 350° oven.

❖ You can double this recipe but do not triple it.

Reverse Hamantashen

Dairy
24 Hamantashen

Chocolate with light-colored filling, these seem the exact opposite of regular Hamantashen. They look pretty served together with the contrasting lightly-browned regular Hamantashen.

❖❖❖

3 cups flour	2 egg yolks
A pinch of salt	1 teaspoon vanilla
1 cup plus 4 tablespoons sugar	**Filling:**
8 teaspoons cocoa	White chocolate candy bars,
1 cup margarine	broken into squares

❖❖❖

1. Mix flour, salt, sugar and cocoa.
2. Cut in margarine until mixture resembles coarse crumbs.
3. Stir in egg yolks and vanilla. Knead until smooth.
4. Cover with plastic wrap or waxed paper and refrigerate for at least one hour.
5. Roll dough on floured surface to $1/4$-inch thickness.
6. Cut out circles with cookie cutter or floured glass.
7. Place one cube of chocolate in the center of each circle. Fold dough around filling to create the triangular shape of Hamantashen.
8. Bake in a 350° oven for 10 minutes.

Old Fashioned Sugar Cookies

Dairy or Parve
6–7 dozen

❖ **Notes** ❖

This recipe was on the back of the Domino sugar package over 30 years ago and I still think it's the best sugar cookie around.

❖❖❖

1 cup sugar	1 teaspoon vanilla
¹/₂ teaspoon salt	3 cups flour
³/₄ cup margarine, softened	1 teaspoon baking powder
1 egg	1 egg white, slightly beaten
1 teaspoon grated lemon rind	

❖❖❖

1. Cream sugar, salt and margarine well.
2. Add egg and beat.
3. Blend lemon rind and vanilla into mixture.
4. Gradually stir flour and baking powder into creamed mixture.
5. Roll to ¹/₈ inch thickness on floured board. Cut out circles with cookie cutters or floured glass.
6. Place cookies on ungreased cookie sheets. Brush with beaten egg white, sprinkle with sugar if desired.
7. Bake in a 350° oven for 12 minutes.

Decorating Glaze

1. Blend 1¹/₂ cups powdered sugar into 1 slightly beaten egg white.
2. Add 1 tablespoon melted margarine, ¹/₈ teaspoon salt and ¹/₂ teaspoon vanilla.
3. Beat until smooth. If glaze is thin, add more powdered sugar.
4. Divide glaze into several parts. Tint as desired with food coloring. Apply glaze to cookies with a spoon or clean paint brush.

Mandel Bread

❖❖❖

$^1/_2$ cup shortening or margarine
1   cup sugar
3   eggs
3   cups flour
1$^1/_4$ teaspoons salt
2   teaspoons baking powder
2   teaspoons vanilla
1   cup nuts, chopped

❖❖❖

1. Cream shortening and sugar.
2. Add eggs, one at a time, beating well after each addition.
3. Mix together flour, salt, and baking powder and add to creamed shortening and sugar.
4. Stir in nuts and vanilla.
5. Mold dough into log-shaped rolls on greased cookie sheets.
6. Bake in a 350° oven for $^1/_2$ hour.
7. Slice logs $^1/_4$-$^1/_2$ inch thick and lay slices on their sides.
8. Reduce oven temperature to 200° and "toast" slices until golden.

Strawberries in Orange Juice

Parve

❖ **Notes** ❖

Lush, ripe strawberries served with fresh orange juice won't need sugar. The colors look lovely together and the taste is unforgettable.

❖❖❖

4   **fresh ripe
            strawberries
            per serving**
$^1/_2$ **cup fresh orange
            juice per
            serving**

❖❖❖

1. Just before serving, wash and hull the strawberries. Place in stemmed glasses or dessert bowls.
2. Pour fresh chilled orange juice over strawberries and serve.

Poached Vanilla Pears

❖ **Notes** ❖

❖❖❖

6   **firm ripe pears**
1   **cup sugar**
1   **cup water**
1   **tablespoon lemon juice**
2   **teaspoons vanilla**

❖❖❖

1. Peel whole pears, leaving stems intact.
2. In a saucepan that will hold all six pears standing upright, combine sugar, water, lemon juice and vanilla. Bring to a boil.
3. Add the pears and cook, covered, for 30 minutes, or until pears are tender but not mushy.
4. Remove from heat and let stand until cool. Refrigerate until well chilled.

Cranberry Ice

Parve
6 servings

Delightfully cool and refreshing.

❖❖❖

2   **16-ounce cans jellied cranberry sauce**
2   **cups lemon-lime soda**
    Garnish: mint sprigs

❖❖❖

1. Beat cranberry sauce on high speed of mixer until very smooth.
2. Gently fold in soda.
3. Pour into four ice-cube trays and freeze.
4. Remove from freezer and beat again until smooth and frothy.
5. Freeze in a 2-quart container until ready to serve. Remove from freezer about $1/2$ hour before serving.
6. Serve garished with mint sprigs.

Chapter Fifteen
PASSOVER

No kosher cookbook would be complete without a section of Passover recipes. Let me suggest that the first thing you do is photocopy these pages and put them away with your Passover items. That way you won't have to worry about using a *chametz* cookbook during Passover — and you won't waste time looking for your Passover recipes either.

There are so many traditions on Passover, that you have to be careful about what recipes you use. For example, those that don't eat *kitniyot* (legumes) on Passover must be careful about rice recipes; while those who don't eat *gebrocht* should be careful about recipes that call for the addition of water to matzo meal. There are even customs concerning the types of matzo one eats; some people only eat hand baked *shemura* matzo, matzo that has been carefully watched from the time the wheat was cut, to make sure no water dropped on it, while others are just as happy with the regular machine matzo.

But, despite all the different customs, at the Seder Table, everyone joins together to remember the experience of the Exodus. Part of that experience is the wondrous plates of food that seem to go on and on, despite the late hour, and drooping eyelids. These memories leave a taste in our mouths and our hearts, which stay with us as long as we live.

Matzo Brei

❖ **Notes** ❖

Everybody has their favorite version of Matzo Brei and their favorite way of eating it. Some like it with cinnamon-sugar, some like it salty, and some like it with jam. This was my grandmother's recipe and my family can't get enough of this on Pesach.

❖❖❖

8   pieces matzo
8   eggs
1 $^1/_2$ teaspoons salt
$^1/_2$ teaspoon pepper
3   tablespoons butter, margarine
         or oil

❖❖❖

1. Break matzo into pieces and soak in warm water until soft (1 minute).
2. Drain thoroughly.
3. Beat eggs and add to matzo.
4. Add salt and pepper.
5. Melt butter or margarine in large frying pan.
6. Add matzo mixture and cook, stirring and turning, until dry and crispy.
7. Turn out onto serving dish.

Haroset

Parve
12 bars

When you make this, don't forget to save enough for the Seder.

❖ **Notes** ❖

❖❖❖

4 **apples**
¹/₂ cup nuts (pecans, walnuts or
 almonds) finely chopped
1 teaspoon cinnamon
¹/₄ cup sweet wine

❖❖❖

Mix all ingredients together.

Dairy or Parve
6 servings

❖ **Notes** ❖

Passover Pineapple Upside-down Cake

❖❖❖

$^1/_4$ **cup margarine, melted**
$^1/_4$ **cup brown sugar, firmly packed**
$^1/_2$ **teaspoon cinnamon**
1 **8-ounce can sliced pineapple, drained**
$^1/_2$ **cup chopped nuts**
1 **package Passover coffee cake mix**

❖❖❖

1. Spread the bottom of an 8-inch round cake pan with melted margarine.
2. Mix brown sugar and cinnamon with topping from packet in the cake mix. Sprinkle on bottom of pan.
3. Arrange pineapple slices over this and sprinkle with chopped nuts.
4. Prepare cake mix as directed and carefully pour batter over pineapple.
5. Bake in a 350° oven for 40 minutes.
6. Immediately loosen sides of cake with a knife and invert to a serving dish.

Date-Nut Bars

Parve
40 bars

❖❖❖

3	eggs, room temperature
1	cup sugar
1	cup matzo meal
$^1/_2$	teaspoon salt
1	cup dates, pitted and chopped
1	cup pecans, chopped
1	cup raisins

❖❖❖

1. Preheat oven to 325°.
2. Grease 9×13-inch baking pan and set aside.
3. Beat eggs well with an electric mixer.
4. Gradually add sugar and continue beating until mixture becomes pale in color.
5. Add matzo meal and salt.
6. Beat thoroughly, then add dates, nuts, and raisins. Beat on low speed until just mixed.
7. Pour into prepared baking pan and bake in a 325° oven for 45 minutes.
8. Cool 15 minutes; cut into 1×2-inch bars.

❖ These bars freeze well.

Chocolate Chiffon Pie

❖❖❖

Crust:
3 egg whites
¹/₄ cup sugar
1 cup water
1¹/₂ teaspoons lemon juice

Filling:
¹/₂ pound parve margarine
1 cup sugar
3 ounces bittersweet chocolate,
   melted and cooled
4 eggs
   Garnish: pecans or almonds

❖❖❖

Crust:
1. Beat egg whites until stiff.
2. Add sugar alternating with lemon juice. Continue beating until stiff and glossy.
3. Spread in 9-inch pie pan and bake in a 275° oven for 1 hour.

Filling:
4. Cream margarine and sugar.
5. Add melted chocolate and blend on low speed.
6. Add eggs, one at a time, beating 5 minutes at high speed after each addition.
7. Spoon into cooled shell, garnish with nuts, and refrigerate.

Kisses

Parve
60 kisses

My family's favorite Passover dessert — if I made 600 of them, it still wouldn't be enough. It's probably the most economical dessert you can serve.

❖❖❖

4	**egg whites**
¹/₄	**teaspoon salt**
1	**cup sugar**
1	**teaspoon vanilla**

❖❖❖

1. Beat egg whites and salt until stiff and dry.
2. Beat in sugar gradually, 2 teaspoons at a time.
3. Add vanilla and beat until mixture holds it shape.
4. Spoon or pipe through pastry tube onto a cookie sheet lined with parchment paper, or a cookie sheet which has been greased and covered with greased brown paper.
5. Bake in a 250° oven for 50 minutes or until golden. Watch carefully the last 10 minutes to make sure they don't turn brown.

❖ This mixture may also be piped out as shells and filled with fruit.

Matzo Cheese Kugel

❖ **Notes** ❖

❖❖❖

6	matzos, broken into large pieces
5	eggs, beaten
1	cup milk
1	pound cottage cheese
1	teaspoon salt
1/4	cup sugar
1	teaspoon cinnamon
3	tablespoons margarine, melted
1	pint sour cream

❖❖❖

1. Combine eggs with milk and beat well.
2. Mix thoroughly with cottage cheese, salt, sugar, cinnamon and melted margarine.
3. In a greased 1 1/2 quart baking dish, arrange three of the matzos.
4. Pour half the cheese mixture over them. Repeat with remaining cheese mixture and matzos.
5. Bake in a 350° oven for 40 minutes or until set.
6. Serve topped with sour cream.

Sweet Potato–Applesauce Pudding

Parve
6 servings

❖❖❖

6   medium sweet potatoes
      (3 pounds)
2   cups applesauce
³/₄ teaspoon cinnamon
³/₄ cup honey
3   tablespoons parve margarine,
      melted
    Sprinkling of chopped pecans
      (optional)

❖❖❖

1. Cook sweet potatoes until soft; peel and slice.
2. Mix applesauce and cinnamon.
3. In a greased 2-quart baking dish, arrange alternate layers of potato and applesauce.
4. Dribble each layer with honey and melted margarine and sprinkle with chopped pecans.
5. Bake, uncovered, in a 350° oven for 45 minutes, basting occasionally.

Baked Squash

❖ **Notes** ❖

❖❖❖

3   **pounds yellow squash or
      zucchini, washed and diced**
$^1/_2$ **cup chopped onion**
$^1/_2$ **cup matzo meal**
2   **eggs**
$^1/_2$ **cup oil or mayonnaise**
1   **tablespoon sugar**
1   **teaspoon salt**
$^1/_2$ **teaspoon pepper**

❖❖❖

1. Combine all ingredients and pour into baking dish.
2. Sprinkle with additional matzo meal.
3. Sprinkle a little oil over top and bake in a 375° oven for about 1 hour or until brown on top.

Spiced Carrots

Parve
4 servings

❖ **Notes** ❖

❖❖❖

1	**pound carrots**
2	**tablespoons honey**
3	**tablespoons parve margarine or oil**
1	**teaspoon cloves**
2	**tablespoons brown sugar**
¹/₂	**teaspoon ground ginger**
	A pinch of salt
	The juice of 1 orange

❖❖❖

1. Peel and slice carrots.
2. Place all ingredients in saucepan, except for cloves and ginger. Cook over low heat for 20 minutes.
3. Add cloves and ginger. Cook, covered, an additional 15 minutes.

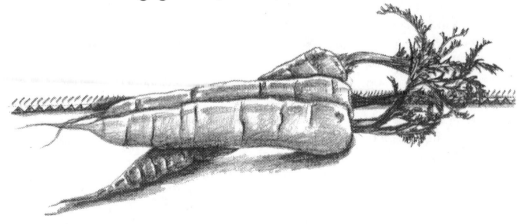

Passover Vegetable Kugel

Parve
8 servings

❖❖❖

2	tablespoons oil
2	large onions, chopped
2	pounds yellow squash, chopped or grated
2	large carrots, chopped or grated
1	pound mushrooms, sliced
2	large potatoes, grated
4	eggs
$1/2$	teaspoon garlic powder
1	tablespoon parsley flakes
$1^1/2$	teaspoons salt
$1/2$	teaspoon pepper
$1/3$	cup matzo meal
	Paprika

❖❖❖

1. Saute onions until soft but not brown.
2. Strain other vegetables, except mushrooms, squeezing to get as much liquid out as possible.
3. Combine onions and vegetables, add eggs, seasoning, salt, pepper and matzo meal.
4. Pour into a well-greased casserole and sprinkle with paprika. Drizzle a little additional oil over casserole and bake in a 350° oven 1 hour or until brown on top.

Baked Chicken with Mushrooms

Meat
4 servings

❖❖❖

1	chicken, cut into pieces
$^1/_2$	teaspoon onion powder
2	cups chicken soup
3	tablespoons parve margarine
$^1/_4$	teaspoon garlic powder
$^1/_4$	pound fresh mushrooms, sliced
3	tablespoons water
2	tablespoons potato starch

❖❖❖

1. Heat margarine in large skillet.
2. Saute chicken until brown. Remove to a baking dish.
3. Add onion powder, garlic powder and soup to oil.
4. Blend water with potato starch until smooth. Gradually add to soup mixture and cook, stirring constantly until thickened.
5. Pour gravy over chicken and add mushrooms.
6. Cover and bake in a 350° oven for 1 hour.

Fluffy Kneidlach (Matzo Balls)

Parve
12 large balls

This makes a fluffy if somewhat irregularly shaped matzo ball. It is a good recipe for those who use shmura matzo meal.

❖❖❖

3   eggs, separated
³/₄   cup matzo meal
¹/₂   teaspoon salt
1   teaspoon parsley flakes

❖❖❖

1. Beat egg whites until stiff.
2. In a separate bowl, beat egg yolks with salt and matzo meal.
3. Gently fold egg whites into matzo meal mixture. Let stand for five minutes.
4. With a spoon, form mixture into balls.
5. Drop into boiling salted water.
6. Cover and cook for 35 minutes.

Chapter Sixteen
SUBSTITUTION MAGIC
AND EQUIVALENTS

One of the most important ingredients of a creative cook is the ability to substitute ingredients. When I started keeping kosher over 20 years ago, I went through all my favorite recipes and threw away the ones that called for non-kosher ingredients, thinking I would never use them again.

To both my delight and dismay (at having thrown away so many of my favorite recipes!), I eventually learned that there are very few recipes that can't be adjusted for a kosher home with absolutely no loss of flavor. All it takes is a little imagination.

For instance, New Orleans is famous for its barbecued shrimp. A delicious version can be created using any firm-fleshed kosher fish, or the relatively new kosher fish that is shaped to look like shrimp.

It's almost always better to substitute than to omit an ingredient. If a recipe calls for oregano and you're out of it, or you don't care for it, substitute basil or another herb, but don't just leave it out.

Use the following charts and your imagination to expand your creativity, your knowledge of cooking, and your repertoire of great tasting meals.